Architect's Job Book

Eighth Edition

RIBA Publishing

© RIBA Enterprises Ltd, 2008
Published by RIBA Publishing, 15 Bonhill Street, London EC2P 2EA

ISBN 978 1 85946 252 2

Stock Code 61857

The right of 3DReid to be identified as the Editor of the Eighth Edition of this Work has been asserted in accordance with the Copyright, Design and Patents Act 1988 Section 77 and 78.

The Seventh Edition of this Work was prepared by Sarah Lupton.

British Library Cataloguing in Publications Data
A catalogue record for this book is available from the British Library.

Publisher: Steven Cross
Commissioning Editor: John Elkington
Project Editor: Anna Waters
Designed and typeset by Ben Millbank
Printed and bound by Latimer Trend, Plymouth

We make every effort to ensure the accuracy and quality of information when it is published. However, we can take no responsibility for the subsequent use of this information, nor for any errors or omissions that it may contain.

RIBA Publishing is part of RIBA Enterprises Ltd. www.ribaenterprises.com

Cover image: Admirals Park, Dartford
Architect: 3DReid
Photograph: © Morley von Sternberg

CONTENTS

Foreword

Through its seven previous editions the *RIBA Architect's Job Book* has become a familiar and highly valued reference tool for the architectural profession.

The *RIBA Architect's Job Book* follows the structure of the well established and widely used work stages of the *RIBA Plan of Work*. It provides stage by stage guidance to assist the architect in managing the building design and procurement process from inception to completion. Set out in a new easy to use format, this eighth edition provides comprehensive information on the administration of an architectural project, with good practice guidance, action checklists and work stage outputs for both traditional and design and build procurement options.

Whatever the stage of your career, the *RIBA Architect's Job Book* will provide an accessible and vital knowledge resource for contemporary architectural practice. I commend this publication to the experienced architect no less than to the student preparing for practice.

Sunand Prasad
President, RIBA

Preface to the Eighth Edition

As with previous editions of the *Architect's Job Book*, the eighth edition is based on the *RIBA Outline Plan of Work*, which was published in 2007 and is now amplified in considerable detail in *Plan of Work: Multi-disciplinary Services* (RIBA Publishing, 2008). From the outset the authors thought it was important to recapture some of the classic features of earlier editions: there has been a return to an A4 format, and efforts have been made to ensure that the structure of the book is simple, consistent and clear. The objective must be that the user is able to navigate through the book easily and quickly find the relevant information.

All the chapters now have the same format and identical subheadings, recognising the iterative nature of design.

This edition is also accompanied by a website – www.ribabookshops.com/jobbook – which contains free downloadable action checklists and template forms, enabling the creation of a project plan for individual projects. This is a conscious effort to recapture the concept of the Job Book as a practical tool, something that inspired earlier editions. The combination of the electronic checklists used in conjunction with the hard copy explanatory notes will enable the original idea to be a realised using modern technology.

Acknowledgements

The authors would like to thank Roland Phillips, Keith Snook and Richard Brindley for their helpful comments on early drafts. They would also like to thank Stuart Barlow, 3DReid's director of sustainability and technology, for his contribution in Stages L2 and L3 as well as in other parts of the book.

About the authors

Robert Dalziel and Nigel Ostime are architects and directors of 3DReid, one of the largest architectural practices in the UK.

They both have broad experience of a wide range of sectors including residential, retail, hotels, offices, airports and industrial buildings as well as mixed-use town centre developments. They also have a keen interest in the process of design and were instrumental in the development of their practice's in-house, 'knowledge-led' approach to project work, an approach that ensures all the necessary information and skills are fed into the design at the right time to optimise efficiency and provide the best solutions consistently across the office.

Robert has contributed to two other books published by RIBA Publishing, *The Commercial Offices Handbook* (2003) and *Space Craft: Developments in Architectural Computing* (2008). He also contributed the architectural content to BCO Guides in 2000 and 2005.

How to use this book

The new eighth edition of the *Architect's Job Book* can be used either on its own or in tandem with the companion website www.ribabookshops.com/jobbook (see below), from which you may download editable electronic documents related to the book, free of charge.

As in the seventh edition, this new edition follows the work stages in the *RIBA Outline Plan of Work* (reproduced here) but otherwise has been completely updated and redesigned for ease of use. The chapters are structured consistently: a general description of the stage and key obligations during it, is followed by a comprehensive action checklist comprising sections on 'Preliminary Issues', 'Stage Activities', 'General Procedures' and 'Stage Outputs'. Throughout, useful 'notes' provide background information and 'watch points'. The action checklists are supported by supplementary material to offer further guidance or to give examples of template forms. As far as possible, actions have been set out in chronological order but the needs and programmes of individual projects will vary, and many actions will of necessity run in parallel. Therefore all the actions in a stage should be reviewed at its outset to ensure their timely execution.

The action checklist for each work stage are intended to be generic. Although they are founded in S-Con-07 from the RIBA's suite of appointment documents, the tasks that may be appropriate or necessary at each stage will vary considerably depending on the context and the nature of the project even when using this form of appointment. It may well be that some actions listed are not necessary in a given situation, or that additional work may be essential. Furthermore, many architects may amend S-Con-07, use a different RIBA form, or use entirely different terms of appointment. The action lists should therefore always be reviewed at the beginning of each specific project and work stage.

The *Architect's Job Book* is not, of course, intended to constitute a quality management system in itself. Nevertheless some parts of it, for example the action checklists and standard forms, may be relevant to an office quality system. It should always be remembered, however, that the *Architect's Job Book* checklists are not comprehensive, and though they may form a useful starting point they must be adapted to the specific needs of a particular practice.

The *Architect's Job Book* is coordinated with and cross-referenced to other RIBA documents and Good Practice Guides, together forming a suite of RIBA-approved practice and guidance references. In particular, the book should be read in conjunction with the *Green Guide to the Architect's Job Book*, second edition, by Sandy Halliday (RIBA Publishing, 2007). The *Green Guide* should always be consulted for a more detailed understanding of how sustainability issues can be incorporated in the work stages.

The companion website – www.ribabookshops.com/jobbook

The companion website has been developed to allow architects to download, free of charge, a comprehensive set of editable template documents to help them to run their projects smoothly and consistently to a high standard. The templates may be completed electronically or printed out and completed manually to suit the preferred method of working. It is envisaged that a set of checklists is used at the start of every new project as the project plan for that job. To use these templates safely and as intended it is important to refer to the introductory and supplemental guidance and background notes in the book.

Once downloaded, the action checklists may be edited electronically, allowing them to form the basis of the project plan. For each action in the checklists it is possible to record the date on which the action was undertaken or completed, and there is also space below to record notes on the activity, if relevant.

The numbering of the action checklists on the companion website mirrors that used in the book. The website also contains all the figures reproduced in the book. Additionally, it includes a number of other template forms and letters for a multitude of purposes; these additional documents are listed separately below.

List of documents available on the companion website

Action checklists

PRE200	Stage Activities	H100	Preliminary Issues
A-B100	Preliminary Issues	H200	Stage Activities
A-B200	Stage Activities	H300	General Procedures
A-B300	General Procedures	H400	Stage Outputs
A-B400	Stage Outputs	J100	Preliminary Issues
C100	Preliminary Issues	J200	Stage Activities
C200	Stage Activities	J300	General Procedures
C300	General Procedures	J400	Stage Outputs
C400	Stage Outputs	K100	Preliminary Issues
D100	Preliminary Issues	K200	Stage Activities
D200	Stage Activities	K300	General Procedures
D300	General Procedures	K400	Stage Outputs
D400	Stage Outputs	L100	Preliminary Issues
E100	Preliminary Issues	L200	Stage Activities
E200	Stage Activities	L400	Stage Outputs
E300	General Procedures		
E400	Stage Outputs		
F100	Preliminary Issues		
F200	Stage Activities		
F300	General Procedures		
F400	Stage Outputs		
G100	Preliminary Issues		
G200	Stage Activities		
G300	General Procedures		
G400	Stage Outputs		

Other documents in the *Architect's Job Book*

Fig. PRE1   Specimen letter to architect formerly engaged on project

Fig. PRE2   Specimen project resource planning sheet

Fig. PRE3   Specimen letter confirming preliminary agreement

Fig. A–B1   Specimen agenda for initial site meeting

Fig. A–B2   RIBA safety code: visits to sites and unoccupied buildings

Fig. C1   Specimen cost plan/budget estimate

Fig. E1   Specimen checklist of necessary drawn information

Fig. E2a   Specimen register of drawings

Fig. E2b   Specimen register of prints

Fig. E3   Specimen schedule of drawings required

Fig. E4   Specimen architect's drawing issue sheet

Fig. E5   Specimen record of drawings received

Fig. E6   Specimen record of design change notice and record

Fig. J1   Specimen agenda for pre-contract meeting

Fig. K1   Specimen financial report to client

Fig. K2   Specimen agenda for architect's site progress meeting

Fig. K3   Specimen report from for predictive site visits

Fig. K4   Specimen record form of architect's instructions issued

Fig. K5   Specimen record of site delays observed

Fig. K6   Specimen record of defective work

Fig. K7   Specimen record form of claims by contractor

Additional documents on the companion website but not in the *Architect's Job Book*

Fig. D1   Room data notes

Fig. H1   Letter of preliminary invitation to tender

Fig. H2   Letter to unsuccessful tenderers for specialist sub-contract works or supply items

Fig. H3   Letter notifying tendered prices for specialist sub-contract works or supply items

Fig. H4   Advance order to named sub-contractor

Fig. H5a   Preliminary invitation to tender for main contract works SBC05

Fig. H5b   Preliminary invitation to tender for main contract works IC05, ICD05

Fig. H5c   Preliminary invitation to tender for main contract works MW05, MWD05

Fig. H6   Invitation to tender for main contract works using Bills of Quantities

Fig. H7   Invitation to tender for main contract works using drawings, specifications and schedules

Fig. H8   Certificate of collusion

Fig. H9   Letter to contractor submitting most acceptable tender

Fig. H10   Letter to contractor submitting second most acceptable tender

Fig. H11   Letter to unsuccessful tenderers

Fig. J2   Letter to contractor notifying early start of the main contract works

Fig. J3   Letter notifying unsuccessful contractors

Fig. J4   Letter to contractor with contract documents for signature

Fig. J5   Letter to employer with contract documents for signature

Fig. J6   Letter to newly appointed Clerk of Works

Fig. K8   Letter in reply to a contractor's unsubstantiated claim

Fig. L1   Record of defects reported after practical completion

RIBA ⚏ Outline Plan of Work 2007

The Outline Plan of Work organises the process of managing, and designing building projects and administering building contracts into a number of key Work Stages. The sequence or content of Work Stages may vary or they may overlap to suit the procurement method (see pages 2 and 3).

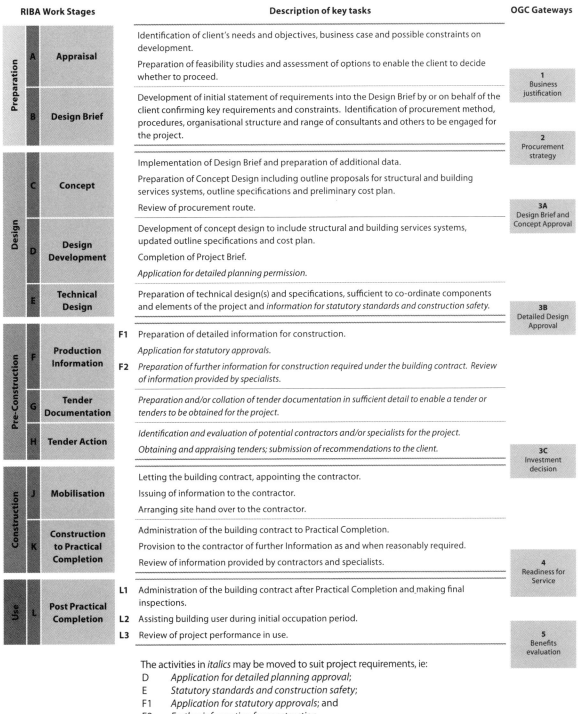

RIBA Work Stages		Description of key tasks	OGC Gateways
Preparation	**A** Appraisal	Identification of client's needs and objectives, business case and possible constraints on development. Preparation of feasibility studies and assessment of options to enable the client to decide whether to proceed.	**1** Business justification
	B Design Brief	Development of initial statement of requirements into the Design Brief by or on behalf of the client confirming key requirements and constraints. Identification of procurement method, procedures, organisational structure and range of consultants and others to be engaged for the project.	**2** Procurement strategy
Design	**C** Concept	Implementation of Design Brief and preparation of additional data. Preparation of Concept Design including outline proposals for structural and building services systems, outline specifications and preliminary cost plan. Review of procurement route.	**3A** Design Brief and Concept Approval
	D Design Development	Development of concept design to include structural and building services systems, updated outline specifications and cost plan. Completion of Project Brief. *Application for detailed planning permission.*	
	E Technical Design	Preparation of technical design(s) and specifications, sufficient to co-ordinate components and elements of the project and *information for statutory standards and construction safety.*	**3B** Detailed Design Approval
Pre-Construction	**F** Production Information	**F1** Preparation of detailed information for construction. *Application for statutory approvals.* **F2** *Preparation of further information for construction required under the building contract. Review of information provided by specialists.*	
	G Tender Documentation	*Preparation and/or collation of tender documentation in sufficient detail to enable a tender or tenders to be obtained for the project.*	
	H Tender Action	*Identification and evaluation of potential contractors and/or specialists for the project. Obtaining and appraising tenders; submission of recommendations to the client.*	**3C** Investment decision
Construction	**J** Mobilisation	Letting the building contract, appointing the contractor. Issuing of information to the contractor. Arranging site hand over to the contractor.	
	K Construction to Practical Completion	Administration of the building contract to Practical Completion. Provision to the contractor of further Information as and when reasonably required. Review of information provided by contractors and specialists.	**4** Readiness for Service
Use	**L** Post Practical Completion	**L1** Administration of the building contract after Practical Completion and making final inspections. **L2** Assisting building user during initial occupation period. **L3** Review of project performance in use.	**5** Benefits evaluation

The activities in *italics* may be moved to suit project requirements, ie:

D   *Application for detailed planning approval;*
E   *Statutory standards and construction safety;*
F1   *Application for statutory approvals; and*
F2   *Further information for construction.*
G+H *Invitation and appraisal of tenders*

RIBA ✠ Outline Plan of Work 2007

Work Stage Sequences by Procurement Method

The diagrams illustrate different sequences for completion of Work Stages for various procurement methods, but are not representative of time.

In arriving at an acceptable timescale the choice of procurement method may be as relevant as other more obvious factors such as the amount of work to be done, the client's tendering requirements, risks associated with third party approvals or funding etc.

✠ This symbol indicates that prior to commencement time should be allowed for appointing consultants.

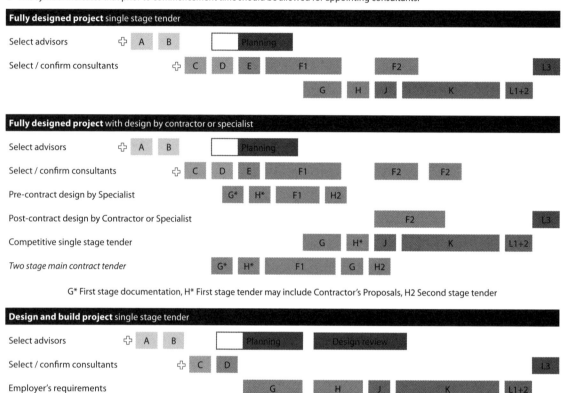

Fully designed project single stage tender

Select advisors — ✠ A B — Planning

Select / confirm consultants — ✠ C D E F1 F2 L3

G H J K L1+2

Fully designed project with design by contractor or specialist

Select advisors — ✠ A B — Planning

Select / confirm consultants — ✠ C D E F1 F2 F2

Pre-contract design by Specialist — G* H* F1 H2

Post-contract design by Contractor or Specialist — F2 L3

Competitive single stage tender — G H* J K L1+2

Two stage main contract tender — G* H* F1 G H2

G* First stage documentation, H* First stage tender may include Contractor's Proposals, H2 Second stage tender

Design and build project single stage tender

Select advisors — ✠ A B — Planning Design review

Select / confirm consultants — ✠ C D — L3

Employer's requirements — G H J K L1+2

Contractor's proposals — E F

Note: final design activity by Client may be at stage C, D, E or possibly F. These stages not repeated by contractor

Design and build project two stage tender (all design by contractor)

Appoint consultants — ✠ A B — Design review L3

Employer's requirements — G H1 H2 J/K L1+2

Contractor's proposals — C D/E F

Planning

Partnering contract

Output specification by client

Appoint consultants — ✠ A B — Planning

Appoint partnering team — H C D E F1 F2

Select specialists — H E F1 F2 L3

Agree guaranteed maximum price — G/H J/K L1+2

Design and construction sequences may be as shown for Management contract / Construction management

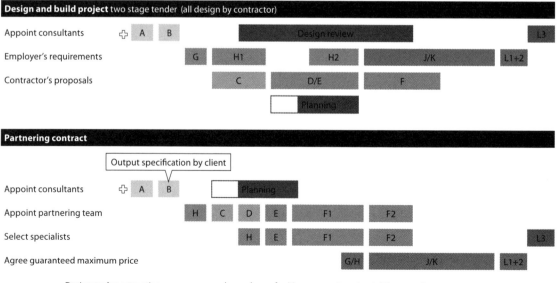

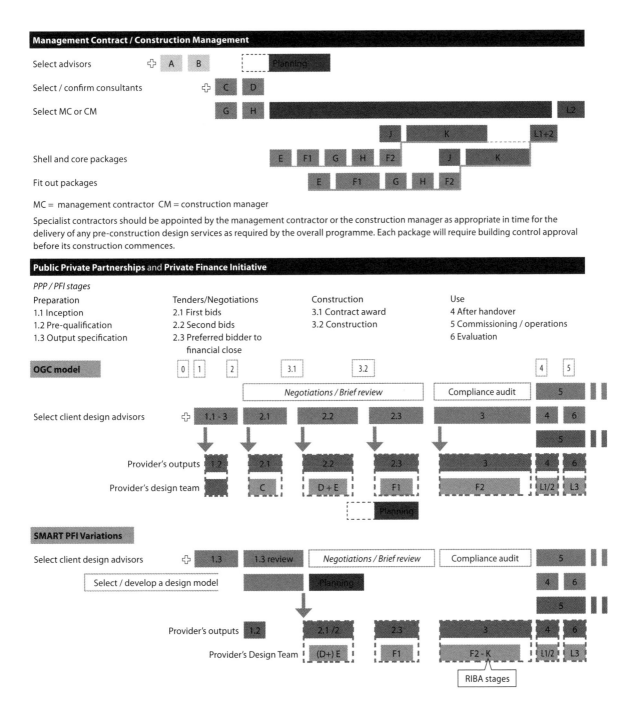

Management Contract / Construction Management

Select advisors — A B — Planning

Select / confirm consultants — C D

Select MC or CM — G H ... L2

J K L1+2

Shell and core packages — E F1 G H F2 J K

Fit out packages — E F1 G H F2

MC = management contractor   CM = construction manager

Specialist contractors should be appointed by the management contractor or the construction manager as appropriate in time for the delivery of any pre-construction design services as required by the overall programme. Each package will require building control approval before its construction commences.

Public Private Partnerships and **Private Finance Initiative**

PPP / PFI stages

Preparation	Tenders/Negotiations	Construction	Use
1.1 Inception	2.1 First bids	3.1 Contract award	4 After handover
1.2 Pre-qualification	2.2 Second bids	3.2 Construction	5 Commissioning / operations
1.3 Output specification	2.3 Preferred bidder to financial close		6 Evaluation

OGC model

0 1 2   3.1   3.2   4 5

Negotiations / Brief review   Compliance audit   5

Select client design advisors — 1.1 - 3 2.1 2.2 2.3 3 4 6

5

Provider's outputs — 1.2 2.1 2.2 2.3 3 4 6

Provider's design team — C D + E F1 F2 L1/2 L3

Planning

SMART PFI Variations

Select client design advisors — 1.3 1.3 review Negotiations / Brief review Compliance audit 5

Select / develop a design model — Planning 4 6

5

Provider's outputs — 1.2 2.1 /2 2.3 3 4 6

Provider's Design Team — (D+) E F1 F2 - K L1/2 L3

RIBA stages

PREPARATION > PRE-AGREEMENT STAGE

Pre-agreement

CONTENTS

Stage Description

Professional services

There is increased potential within the industry for the architect to perform a wide variety of roles. Great care is therefore needed to secure any commission on the right basis as it can no longer always be assumed that 'the normal services will apply', or that there will be a common understanding between architect and client as to what the 'normal services' might mean.

In any individual case the services will vary according to the expectations and requirements of the client. They will usually relate to a specific building project; however, they could be in the form of general advice or consultancy work, in fields such as conservation, premises management, environmental or access auditing, or corporate image design or development.

If relating to a specific project the services will be affected by the nature and scale of the building project, the management structure set up for the project, and by the procurement method adopted. The architect could be engaged from inception through to completion, or perhaps for specific services at a single stage. Given this wide diversity of potential roles, it is important that the services to be provided in each case are identified accurately and with care.

The job or commission can be secured through a variety of methods. For example, it could be as a result of a direct approach made to a potential client or an invitation to discuss and negotiate or to bid in competition. This might concern only the architect, or it might call for a joint submission with other professionals or partners from commerce and industry.

Where securing a commission is subject to competitive tendering, it is essential to know what criteria the client intends to apply when evaluating tenders, and what procedures will govern the submission. A careful assessment of resources required will be crucial in order to make realistic costings and establish viability before tendering.

Whatever the method of securing the commission, the importance of having an agreement in writing cannot be emphasised enough. It is a requirement of both the RIBA and the ARB Codes of Conduct, and it is normal practice to use one of the standard forms published by the RIBA. If these are not used then great care must be taken to allow for the effect of legislation which directly regulates many aspects of an architect's appointment, particularly payment provisions and dispute resolution.

Sometimes, where the architect is contacted at a very early stage, the nature of the project and the scope of the services required may be so unclear that it is not practicable to use one of the standard forms. In these cases it may be better to agree the preliminary services by letter, but it is essential that the services are confirmed in writing.

A successful working relationship depends on the roles of all parties being established clearly from the outset, and without the ambiguities that so frequently lead to misunderstandings and conflict. The activities listed below could be relevant before the appointment of an architect, whether for full or partial services, under any Plan of Work stage or part of a stage, and are generally applicable regardless of procurement method.

PRE200	**Stage Activities**

PRE210	**Initial discussions**

ACTION **PRE211**	Prepare and activate strategy to target potential clients. This may include a practice statement.	SEE ALSO **PRE/SM1**

ACTION **PRE212**	Respond at once to approaches from potential clients. If it is of interest, ask for further particulars, including details of the selection process to be adopted. Establish as much as possible by telephone or in writing.	SEE ALSO **PRE/SM2**
NOTE	*Avoid spending unnecessary time on 'long shots' or unsuitable commissions. The client should be able to explain enough of what they have in mind, particularly with regard to how they feel an architect may be able to help them, to establish whether a meeting would be worthwhile. In particular, avoid being drawn into giving free advice.*	

ACTION **PRE213**	Arrange a preliminary meeting, if appropriate, to discuss requirements.
	The initial meetings between client and architect will set the tone for the future working relationship. Clarify your respective roles and responsibilities.
	Consider your reaction to the client and the project.
	Are you in general sympathy with the client's needs and aspirations – if not, will this have an adverse effect on your work? Are the prospects good for building up a good understanding with the client? This is the stage at which key issues of a philosophical or political nature can be raised, such as the client's level of concern regarding environmental issues, or their interest and involvement in new procurement approaches such as partnering.
(CONTINUES)	Be properly equipped with information about your practice and its work.

ACTION **PRE213** CONTINUED	Remember that a professional appointment is a process of mutual selection: have ready a practice brochure with details of the practice's track record and personnel and a truthful statement about its expertise, experience and resources.
NOTE	*Take care when offering professional advice gratuitously to friends and acquaintances. The duty of care that you owe is not related to the size of fee. Even if there is no fee, you might still have a duty in tort.*
	Do not be casual in your dealings and inadvertently let yourself in for more than you intended. Under certain circumstances informal dealings can be construed as giving rise to contractual relationships. A contractual duty, if breached, could result in loss and an ensuing claim.
	Warn the client at once if design requirements, timing and budget seem unrealistic. Remember that a failure to warn could leave you open to allegations of negligence. Explain fully what you advise should be done. Avoid jargon, and take care not to seem patronising or arrogant.
ACTION **PRE214**	Identify the client, and the status and authority of any client representative.
	Note whether an individual is acting in a private capacity or representing a charitable organisation, consortium or a company, etc. If a representative, then what authority is he or she acting under and with what power?
	In the case of a commercial or industrial client, make certain precisely where the ultimate authority resides. For example, the client's company might exist within a parent body. If the company fails and is unable to pay your fees, the benefits of your work could still be available to the parent body, which might have no legal obligation for the unpaid fees.
	Where the client is a couple (married or unmarried), or a group of individuals who have formed some kind of association, be sure that you know who has authority to make decisions, give instructions and sign cheques.

ACTION **PRE215**	Check whether the project is for direct occupation by the client or more in the nature of a speculative venture. Enquire about the possible involvement of a user client who may expect to be consulted.
NOTE	*Bear in mind that working with a group of people on a community – type project, or one which involves a user client, may entail a great deal of extra work, some of it outside normal working hours.*

ACTION **PRE216**	Check the experience of the client. Some clients know exactly what is needed and what they can realistically expect from consultants, while some may never have built before – this may be a once-in-a-lifetime experience.
NOTE	*Be particularly careful in initial meetings with inexperienced clients. Remember that your legal duty of care can relate to the known experience or inexperience of your client.*

ACTION **PRE217**	Check the soundness of the client. Make discreet enquiries about the prospective client's business record, and apparent financial position. Is there any known tendency to questionable business dealings or hasty resort to threats of legal action? What nature of client are they? What previous projects have they commissioned? What were they like to work with?

ACTION **PRE218**	Check whether any other architects were formerly involved with the project. If so, check that their appointment has been properly terminated and notify them in writing of your own appointment, when this has been formally concluded. Fig. PRE 1 is a specimen letter.	SEE ALSO **Fig. PRE1**

PRE220	Bidding for the Project

ACTION **PRE221**	Check the client's requirements for the submission. If involved in competitive fee bidding, make sure that it is on fair and equitable terms, and that the given information is sufficient to permit preparation of a realistic bid. Confirm in writing any reservations or requests for further information.	SEE ALSO **PRE/SM2**
ACTION **PRE222**	Agree a common policy between fellow consultants if the fee bid is to be a team effort. Agree compatible working methods, procedures, and information format.	
ACTION **PRE223**	Assess carefully what the project will require in terms of practice resources before you quote a fee. Do you have the necessary skills and staff? Can they be made available for the particular programme? If it looks as if you will be overstretched, can you buy in skills or sublet work? Fig. PRE2 is a project resource planning sheet. Whether prepared manually or as a spreadsheet, this could provide essential information for a fee bid and be a tool for monitoring small jobs.	SEE ALSO **Fig.PRE2**
ACTION **PRE224**	Decide whether it is realistic to undertake the commission with confidence that the timetable, quality of services and budget can be met. What are the risks, and can they be traded off against likely benefits to the practice if the commission is won?	
ACTION **PRE225**	Identify the likely role and nature of professional services needed. Will you be acting as lead consultant, as design leader, as a consultant team member, as consultant to the Employer Client in design and build, as provider of information to the Contractor Client in design and build, or even as coordinator or manager for separate trades contracts? Make an appraisal and consider carefully the implications.	SEE ALSO **PRE/SM3**
ACTION **PRE226** NOTE	Examine carefully any terms or conditions proposed by the client. *Be wary of conditions which might imply a level of services beyond that which can be reasonably provided for the fee.*	

| ACTION
PRE227 | Check that there is no conflict with professional Codes. |

| ACTION
PRE228 | Consider whether the terms and conditions follow normal practice or whether there is specially drafted wording which shows considerable client bias. |

| ACTION
PRE229 | Check what the client has asked for concerning indemnities, third party warranties, liability period, levels of professional indemnity cover, etc. and consider whether these are reasonable or acceptable. If being considered for the commission depends on evidence of PII cover well in excess of that presently arranged, discuss with insurers the possibility of providing such cover as an interim measure, with the certainty of extending it if and when the commission is secured. |

| NOTE | *Take expert advice from a construction lawyer and insurers if the client seeks to impose onerous conditions.* |

PRE230 Design and build

| ACTION
PRE231 | When acting for Contractor Clients in design and build, establish who carries the liability for design and to what extent. The contractor might not be insured against failures of design, and the liability might extend beyond the normal professional duty to exercise reasonable skill and care. |

ACTION
PRE232

When acting for Employer Clients in design and build, be wary if asked to check the Contractor's Proposals against the Employer's Requirements, and avoid 'approving' drawings submitted by contractor or sub-contractors.

NOTE

Take expert advice on whether terms proposed by the client comply with current legislation, unless it is clear that they follow those currently recommended by the RIBA. It is particularly important to check that terms regarding payment, notices and dispute resolution comply with the Housing Grants, Reconstruction and Development Act, and that a provision to deal with the Contracts (Rights of Third Parties) Act has been incorporated.

Remember that the law requires a professional to exercise reasonable skill and care. Resist any attempt to get you to guarantee what might not be attainable, e.g. that a building will be 'fit for the purpose intended'.

Do not enter into collateral agreements with third parties or give indemnities which impose greater liabilities than those which arise out of the agreement already entered into with your client.

ACTION
PRE233

If no terms are stipulated, draw up terms of appointment that could be proposed.

Consider the minimum and maximum level of services which might be appropriate for the project, but in order to remain competitive keep strictly within the stated requirements when compiling the proposal.

NOTE

Use a Standard Form of Appointment prepared by the RIBA, exactly as recommended in the guidance notes. If for some reason this is not possible, take expert advice on the terms to be proposed.

NOTE

When setting out in writing the professional services you agree to carry out, make absolutely clear what is not included. Leave no room for misunderstandings, particularly when dealing with new or inexperienced clients.

NOTE

With a consumer client, always arrange to meet and talk through the terms proposed in detail, and make sure your client fully understands them, otherwise under the Unfair Terms in Consumer Contracts Regulations 1994 certain terms may not be considered 'individually negotiated' and therefore become void.

PRE240 Negotiating terms

ACTION
PRE241

Respond to the client with the fee proposal, and be prepared to negotiate if appropriate.

Price the client's stated requirements at the outset, no more and no less. You will need to be competitive, but if you quote a fee that is unrealistically low it might mean that you have to cut corners and the quality of service you are able to provide will suffer accordingly. There are obvious risks in putting yourself under this kind of pressure.

Take the time and trouble to explain fully to a client what you are proposing and why. For example, statutory obligations and necessary consents, production information, and procedures for appointing contractor and sub-contractors may well seem daunting to the uninitiated. It is also sometimes wise to spell out the obvious – for example, that there is no such thing as a maintenance-free building and that regular and adequate maintenance is assumed when designing.

NOTE *Be realistic when negotiating. A successful negotiator knows how far to go and when to stop. The aim should never be to secure a commission at any price.*

PRE250 Finalising the appointment

ACTION
PRE251

Decide whether to accept the commission if offered and confirm it in writing.

ACTION **PRE252**	Submit appointment documents for signature before commencing work. Ensure that future review of the appointment is covered in case it is required. Where a standard form is used, follow the guidance notes exactly.

SEE ALSO
Fig.PRE3

Should it prove premature to enter into a formal Memorandum at this point, when for example the extent of professional involvement cannot yet be determined, then enter into a preliminary agreement as an interim measure, clearly identified as such (see Fig. PRE3).

Keep adequate and appropriate records of all dealings connected with the project. Never sacrifice proper paperwork for the sake of assumed goodwill. File everything systematically, whether in hard copy or in digital form, so that items can be easily found and retrieved. It is essential to have fail-safe back-up arrangements to protect both work in progress and records which may be needed for future reference.

NOTE

Never assume that the commission is won until you have received written confirmation of acceptance.

Supplementary Material

PRE/SM1: Practice statement

Architects intending to approach, or who are being approached by, new clients need to have information about their practice ready to hand. General information might be immediately accessible from a practice brochure, or from entries in the *RIBA Directory of Practices*. In some cases where the practice has a quality management system, the quality manual will contain much relevant information and could be issued to the client. Detailed information required in the context of a particular project might need to be specially assembled. Some client bodies may require all this information in a specific format, but nearly all will expect information to be included about the following:

- practice name, addresses, telephone, fax, e-mail
- status of practice: whether sole principal, partnership, company, etc.
- directors or partners: names, CVs, photos
- practice quality management systems, QA status
- practice health and safety policy
- practice environmental policy
- specialist skills in-house
- practice computer systems
- professional indemnity insurance arrangements (subject to insurer's agreement)
- building type experience
- recent commissions: details, illustrations, contact names
- overseas experience and completed commissions, if relevant
- languages in which the practice is fluent, if relevant
- consultants with whom the practice normally collaborates
- team being offered for the particular commission, with brief CVs

PRE/SM2: Selection process

The appointment of an architect may be handled directly by the client or indirectly through a project manager acting on the client's behalf. It could be for the full traditional services where the architect is lead consultant, or for a limited appointment where the architect might be engaged as design leader or simply to take on a design concept role. Regardless of the nature of the appointment or the procurement method adopted, the selection of an architect is likely to follow one of the following recognised procedures.

One-to-one negotiation

The architect is chosen on the basis of personal contact or recommendation, perhaps after a series of interviews. This procedure includes the following features:

- It is suitable for any project.
- It is particularly suitable where services required are not yet formulated or the initial brief is still unclear.
- The client can have the opportunity of professional help in preparing an initial brief.
- Negotiations over services, terms and fees can be carried out using a standard schedule of services as a focus for discussion.

Competitive interview

The architect is chosen primarily on the basis of a presentation to some stipulated form. The main features include:

- Suitable for projects of any size.
- A limited number of architects are invited to make presentations.
- The architect can expect the client to supply a broad outline of the project and to state exactly what the presentation should cover.
- The presentation can be in written form only, or involve an interview, as stipulated by the client in the invitation. Any design content will not normally extend beyond broad concepts.
- After the presentation, the preferred firm can negotiate services and fees, etc.

Qualifications-based selection

The architect is chosen primarily on the basis of quality, by which meant technical qualifications, design and performance potential and general suitability for the project in question. Refer to the RIBA publication *Guidance for Clients on Quality Based Selection*. The Guidance includes quality assessment forms and score sheets that can be used in the selection process.

After appropriate advertisement an initial list of firms is compiled from which a short list is invited for interview and discussion. The short-list firms are then ranked in order of preference. There is no mention of fees until the preferred firm is selected. If it proves impossible to agree a 'fair and reasonable' fee, negotiations with that firm are irrevocably terminated and fresh negotiations begin with the next preferred firm.

Quality/price selection

The system proposed by the CIB is similar to the above method but involves balancing quality/price at the outset. A ratio is agreed depending on the nature of the project, and indicative ratios are given as follows:

Type of process	Quality/price ratio
Feasibility studies and investigation	85/15
Innovative projects	80/20
Complex projects	70/30
Straightforward projects	50/50
Repeat projects	20/80

Quality criteria are then set out and weighted (note if EC directives apply these will affect how this should be done). Submitted tenders are then assessed for quality by marking each of the quality criteria and summing the marks using the agreed weightings to give a total quality score. Candidates meeting an agreed threshold are then interviewed and their quality score adjusted. Their fees are then examined; the lowest is given a score of 100 and the others score 100 minus the percentage their fee is above the lowest fee. The final quality/price assessment is achieved by multiplying the quality and price scores by the quality/price ratio and adding them together to give a total score out of 100. The highest scoring candidate is awarded the contract.

Fee tender (without design)

The architect is chosen solely on the basis of the fee quoted, that is, the procedure is geared to the competitiveness of the fee.

- Unlikely to be suitable for more complex projects, and those under £500,000 capital value.
- A limited number of firms (say five or six) who accept invitations are sent tender documents. All must receive identical information.
- The information should state precisely which services are required and include an initial brief for the project.
- The tender may comprise a fee quotation and a resources schedule or other specified information.

- After receipt of satisfactory tenders, the client can be expected to enter into an agreement. There is little scope for negotiation architects are required to act fairly and honestly with potential clients and competitors [3.4 of the *RIBA Code of Professional Conduct*].

Fee tender (without design) using the Two Envelope System

The architect is chosen both on the basis of technical qualifications and on a fee quoted. Each is considered separately.

- Unlikely to be suitable for projects of less than £500,000 capital value.
- A limited number of firms (say five or six) who accept invitations are sent tender documents. All must receive identical information.
- The information should state precisely which services are required and include an initial brief for the project.
- The criteria to be used when evaluating the tenders should be stated.
- Two envelopes will normally be provided for tender submissions, clearly marked:

  (1) 'Qualifications' (the technical submission)
  (2) 'Fee' (the tender and quoted figure in a form stipulated by the client)

The Qualifications envelopes are opened first and the firms placed in order of preference. Then the Fee envelope from the preferred tenderer (only) is opened in the presence of that firm. Negotiation might subsequently be needed to arrive at a fair and reasonable figure. The second envelopes of the other firms should remain sealed and be returned to those firms if negotiations are successful. Undertaking 3.3 of the RIBA Code of Professional Conduct must be observed. Only in the event of failure to reach a satisfactory outcome should the Fee envelope of the next preferred tenderer be opened.

Design submission with fee proposal

The architect is chosen both on the basis of a design submission and on a fee quoted. Each is considered separately under the Two Envelope System as described above.

- Suitable for larger projects (e.g. over £1 million).
- A limited number of firms (say three) who accept invitations are sent tender documents. All must receive full identical information.
- The information should state precisely which services are required and include an initial brief for the project.
- Clients should expect to pay a fee to all tenderers who submit detailed design ideas, and this will usually restrict the number of invitations. Architects taking part in such an arrangement would be wise to secure a formal agreement

with the client to this effect.
• Two envelopes will normally be provided for tender submissions, clearly
marked:

(1) 'Design Proposals'
(2) 'Fee Tender'

The Design Proposals envelopes from each of the tenderers is opened first
and the firms placed in order of preference. Then the Fee envelope from the
preferred tenderer (only) is opened. Negotiation might subsequently be needed
to arrive at a fair and reasonable figure. The second envelopes of the other
firms should remain sealed and be returned to those firms if negotiations are
successful. Undertaking 3.3 of the RIBA Code of Professional Conduct must be
observed. Only in the event of failure to reach a satisfactory outcome should
the Fee envelope of the next preferred tenderer be opened.

Design ideas competition

The architect is chosen solely on the basis of design ideas. The procedure does
not involve fee tenders, for the fee is stated in the competition conditions.

• Suitable, in theory, for important projects regardless of size. In practice,
application is likely to be restricted by the relatively high cost to both client
and architect.
• The architect can expect the client to provide a project brief, to define the
professional services required, and to appoint a panel of assessors. This requires
a professional input on the part of the client.
• Competition may be restricted to invited participants, and architects taking
part in such an arrangement can expect to be paid a fee. A formal agreement
with the client to that effect is advisable.
• Competition may be open but there is obviously a high cost risk for architects
who participate.

Competitions are best run to procedures fully set out in Architectural Competitions,
an RIBA code of practice. Undertaking 3.5 of the RIBA Code of Professional
Conduct prohibits architects from entering competitions which the RIBA has
declared to be unacceptable. Guidance on architects' fees may be found in
A Client's Guide to Engaging an Architect, published by the RIBA in 1999.

PRE/SM3: Outline of possible roles for the architect

Some of the more common roles for the architect are described below, with a brief summary of the likely duties under such a role. The detailed duties will be as set out in the appointment documents, and the Plan of Work can be used as a model when discussing the services to be provided.

A standard appointing document should preferably be used but this should never be sent 'cold' to a client. It should first form a focus for discussion on the professional services which need to be commissioned, and only then be completed as a formal confirmation of what has been agreed.

If a preliminary appointment is needed pending formal agreement about the full services to be provided, a letter can be used incorporating the appropriate references. A letter activating appointment for specific stages can often be used in conjunction with a formal appointing document. A variation in services already formally agreed, or additional services to be provided, can often be imported by a letter supplementing the original document. It is important to be meticulous over such matters, however, and to take legal advice where appropriate.

Appointment of architect as design leader, or lead consultant

The architect will normally act as design leader and as such is responsible for coordinating and integrating the work of other design consultants and specialists. Although design management has emerged as a separate skill, and design managers are present as independently appointed consultants on some larger projects, the management and coordination of design information from all sources throughout the process should, in general, be regarded as a key component of the architect's role.

In the traditional or conventional appointment, and particularly on smaller projects, the architect will combine this role with that of lead consultant and contract administrator. On larger projects, the architect's commission is increasingly being confined to certain Plan of Work stages, or designated activities not necessarily to a Plan of Work format. Sometimes, particularly in construction management procurement arrangements, the role will be that of lead consultant working under a project manager who is the first point of contact for the client, and may take on the role of contract administrator. Sometimes the appointment will be for full services, but moving stage by stage. With arrangements where a more flexible approach to appointment is necessary, particular care is needed.

Typical duties

Typical duties of an architect acting as design leader might include:

- directing the design process
- consulting the client about significant design issues
- informing the client of duties under the CDM Regulations
- investigating the feasibility of the requirements, and reporting
- advising the client about any limitations on the use of land or buildings
- preparing outline proposals, a scheme design, detail design drawings, etc
- advising on the need for statutory and other consents, and preparing sufficient information for applications to be made
- preparing sufficient production information for consultants and specialists to develop their proposals, coordinating these and integrating them into the overall scheme
- bringing contract documentation to a final state for inviting tenders

If the architect is also lead consultant and contract administrator, the following might be added:

- advising on the need for and appointment of other consultants
- coordinating the work of other consultants
- advising on methods of procurement, and on tendering and the appointment of the main contractor
- administering the terms of the building contract and inspecting as relevant the performance of the contractor
- issuing further reasonably necessary information, issuing empowered instructions, and acting as certifier as the contract requires, including issue of the final certificate
- arranging for the preparation of record information and manuals

Appointment of architect as consultant in design and build

A majority of design and build contracts, with the possible exception of package deals, involve an architect. This is a role quite different from that with the traditional commission, in that the architect acts solely as consultant to either an Employer Client or a Contractor Client at any one time. It is not uncommon for the architect to be engaged by both, but this would be sequential, never simultaneous, and would entail either the so-called consultant switch or novation. Even under this kind of arrangement it is often extremely difficult to separate clearly legal accountability and design responsibility. The degree of involvement with either Employer or Contractor will vary depending on the particular arrangements. An architect has no stated function in connection with the building contract.

Typical duties – Employer Client

Typical duties of an architect appointed as consultant to an Employer Client might include:

- advising on the initial brief
- informing the Employer Client of duties under the CDM Regulations
- carrying out a site appraisal
- advising on the appointment of other consultants
- advising on and taking part in discussions with statutory and other bodies
- preparing outline proposals and making application for outline planning permission
- advising on development of the brief for the Employer's Requirements
- developing design concept drawings as appropriate for the Employer's Requirements
- advising on tendering procedures
- advising on contract matters
- examining the Contractor's Proposals, including design and the contract sum analysis, and offering advice
- acting as the Employer's Agent under the contract during the construction of the works
- visiting the site during construction and reporting back to the Employer Client;
- advising the Employer Client on his or her obligations under the contract, and assisting in the drafting of statements
- inspecting the works on behalf of the client prior to practical completion and advising the Employer Client
- checking the contractor's as built drawings and operating/maintenance manuals
- advising the Employer Client on the Employer's Final Account and Employer's Final Statement as appropriate

Typical duties – Contractor Client

Typical duties of an architect appointed as consultant to a Contractor Client might include:

- examining the Employer's Requirements and all available information, and discussing a strategy for tendering
- visiting the site, and noting all relevant constraints
- checking arrangements for compliance with the CDM Regulations
- advising on the appointment of other consultants
- checking with authorities on statutory consents obtained and required
- advising on the need for specialist sub-contractors
- fulfilling the role of design leader

- providing the Contractor Client with sketches, specification notes, etc. for initial tendering purposes
- advising about limitations or inconsistencies in the Employer's Requirements
- providing the Contractor Client with drawings, specifications, samples, etc. to support the Contractor's Proposals
- after the contract has been awarded, developing and amending drawings and other documents in the Contractor's Proposals for contract documentation;
- developing design details
- applying for statutory and other necessary approvals
- preparing performance specifications and other detailed information for sub-contractor tendering
- preparing production information drawings, details, schedules, specification notes for the Contractor Client
- inspecting work during construction and reporting to the Contractor Client
- preparing additional drawings, etc as necessary for submission to the Employer in the event of change orders
- visiting manufacturers' workshops/factories as necessary and reporting to the Contractor Client
- assisting in the preparation of as built drawings, operating/maintenance manuals, etc
- inspecting the works prior to practical completion and advising the Contractor Client

Appointment of architect as project manager

The project manager is the individual or firm primarily employed to look after the client's interests throughout the stages of a project in collaboration with the consultant team, including the cost consultant. The project manager's remit can be very wide, ranging from initially managing the brief through to managing the marketing or disposal of the completed project.

The project manager is usually responsible for the overall direction of the consultant team, specialists, contractor and sub-contractors. Administering the contract might be undertaken by the project manager or by a contract administrator working in close collaboration. The project manager's duties will vary considerably according to the nature of the project and the wording of the contract. The appointment of a project manager might be appropriate in traditional procurement, design and build, or for a management contract.

The role of project manager, for which some architects might well have the skills and aptitude, should be seen as separate and distinct from the architect's traditional role. It should not be confused with what many architects think of simply as managing the project.

Typical duties

Typical duties of an independent project manager might include:

- assisting in the preparation and development of the brief
- informing the client of duties under the CDM Regulations
- arranging for feasibility studies and reports
- arranging for measures required by health and safety legislation
- preparing the project management structure and plan
- advising on the procurement method
- arranging the appointment of consultants and specialists
- checking professional indemnity insurances, warranties, etc
- instructing consultants on feasibility studies, research, surveys
- coordinating the design process
- preparing and maintaining an overall cost plan
- organising communication and information systems
- arranging consultations/negotiations with statutory bodies
- arranging monthly reports to the client on cost and completion forecasts
- monitoring the performance, etc. of the consultant team
- arranging tender documentation
- organising pre-qualification checks on contractors
- evaluating tenders and preparing recommendations
- participating in the selection and appointment of the contractor
- arranging for the appointment of a construction supervisor/client's agent
- assembling contract documentation
- arranging for the appointment of an adjudicator and services as required
- issuing instructions and variation orders
- issuing extensions of time notices
- preparing valuations and monitoring the budget
- arranging commissioning and witness tests
- developing a maintenance programme and staff training
- organising handover/occupation procedures
- issuing the practical completion certificate, preparing the final account
- organising maintenance manuals and as built information
- planning facilities management
- advising on the marketing/disposal of the project
- checking that defects are remedied, issuing the final certificate

The employment of an independent project manager who is not the architect is increasingly common on larger projects. In these cases it is important that the delineation of responsibilities as between the architect and the project manager is very clear, both as it is documented in their respective contracts of appointment, and also as it is understood and practised in day-to-day working relationships.

Appointment of architect as construction manager

The construction manager is the individual or organisation employed primarily to manage the construction stages of the project in collaboration with the consultant team, including the cost consultant. The appointee will be a specialist with contracting experience, paid by fee, and should preferably be appointed early (at the same time as the consultant team) so that he or she can participate in initial discussions. However, in practice the construction manager is often not brought in until the pre-construction stages are well advanced. Construction of the project is carried out by trades contractors, each having a direct contract with the employer but working under the direction of the construction manager. Alternatively, the construction manager may enter into a management contract with the employer, and each trade contractor will then enter into a separate 'Works' contract with the construction manager. If the architect is to undertake this role, he or she would usually set up a company specifically for this purpose.

Services that can be provided by a construction manager are held by some people to include helping to establish the client's requirements at pre-construction stages. A construction manager may certainly make a positive contribution at project design stage, but duties will vary considerably according to the nature of the project, the timing of the appointment and the wording of the contract.

Typical duties

Typical duties of a construction manager might include:

- arranging for meetings at design stages between client, consultant team and proposed trades contractors who will have a design responsibility
- recommending the most economical materials and methods to meet the requirements of specification and sound construction practice
- commenting on project drawings and project specification as appropriate, and advising on production information for issue by trades contractors
- advising the consultant team on the division of the project into trades contracts
- advising on the need for works at pre-construction stages, e.g. exploratory, mock-ups, tests of particular components, etc
- arranging as appropriate for checks of the outline cost plan, the preparation of a project cost plan and cash flow forecasts
- advising on measures necessary to satisfy statutory obligations, liaising with local and statutory authorities about construction and on site matters, and monitoring compliance by trades contractors
- preparing a project programme showing lead times for trades contracts;
- preparing detailed week-by-week programmes, and expanding and updating these during the progress of the works

- advising the client on insurances to be taken out in respect of the project
- preparing a schedule of tender events showing earliest start and anticipated finishing dates for all trades contracts
- preparing, in consultation with the consultant team, a suitable tender list of trades contractors, checking references and resource capability
- advising on tender procedures and participating in interviews, together with the client and consultant team as appropriate
- evaluating tenders and preparing recommendations
- advising the client on materials or plant to be ordered prior to placing trades contracts
- arranging for adequate information for setting out, and coordinating this as necessary
- issuing empowered instructions to trades contractors
- receiving, reviewing and coordinating information, shop drawings, etc from trades contractors in consultation with the consultant team
- providing management, administration and planning of trades contracts operations; monitoring methods, progress and quality
- coordinating trades contracts operations in line with the project plan
- arranging regular meetings with trades contractors to monitor progress and ascertain information requirements; chairing regular site meetings, issuing minutes and providing the client with monthly reports
- preparing valuations and dealing with applications for payment from trades contractors
- preparing interim and final accounts for each trade contractor
- issuing certificates as required by the contract, including practical completion, in consultation with the consultant team
- arranging for commissioning and testing
- checking that defects are remedied
- obtaining from each trade contractor relevant records, as built drawings and operating/maintenance manuals

Acting in the role of the construction manager is unlikely to interest the majority of architects directly, as they will only rarely have the necessary experience, skills and aptitude at least as far as projects of any size are concerned. Architects involved in this kind of procurement method are more likely to be acting as designer or lead consultant under the direction of the construction manager.

However, architects sometimes find themselves handling smaller projects where there is no main contractor and the work is carried out by direct labour, sometimes volunteers, or through a series of separate trades contracts. If asked to organise such operations they might be acting as the construction manager with all the attendant responsibilities for setting up the site, programming and coordination. This situation is not covered by standard appointing documents, and it would be well to check with insurers before undertaking to provide this kind of consultancy service. An appropriately drafted agreement would be needed.

Appointment of architect as CDM Coordinator (CDMC)

Under The Construction (Design and Management) Regulations 2007 the client in most jobs will be under a statutory duty to appoint a CDMC and a principal contractor.

Architects might wish to consider appointment as a CDMC either on a job where they are also acting as the architect or one where architectural services are provided by others. In all cases an appointment as CDMC should be seen as distinct from the provision of architectural services and the RIBA publishes a suitable Form of Appointment.

The CDMC will need a sound knowledge of design and construction processes and practice, and of health and safety matters relevant to the particular project. The appointment is to be made as soon as is practicable after the client has sufficient information about the project to be able to assess the appointee's competence and adequacy of resources for health and safety.

Typical duties

Typical duties of an independent CDMC might include:

- informing the client of duties under the CDM Regulations
- advising the client on the competence and resources of designers as relevant to health and safety obligations
- issuing statutory notices to the Health and Safety Executive
- ensuring so far as is reasonably possible that potential hazards are identified, eliminated or reduced at design stages
- ensuring that all consultant team members and others contributing to the design (e.g. specialists/sub-contractors) cooperate over health and safety obligations;
- managing the flow of health and safety information between clients, designers and contractors
- attending pre-tender meetings with invited principal contractors to check adequacy of resources for health and safety obligations, and written health and safety policy statements
- advising the client on the competence and resources of contractors relevant to health and safety obligations
- checking that the principal contractor is provided with reasonably necessary health and safety information before construction commences
- appraising the principal contractor's initial construction phase Health and Safety Plan and advising the client

- monitoring the principal contractor's development of, or changes to, the construction phase plan following variations or additional work, and advising the client as necessary
- observing the principal contractor's compliance with the construction phase plan during construction of the works, and advising the client if there are departures
- obtaining necessary information for the Health and Safety File during the design and construction stages
- preparing the Health and Safety File and advising the client on its safe keeping and future use

The role of CDMC is one which on major projects might be undertaken by an independently appointed architect who has undergone the necessary training. On simpler projects the architect as lead consultant might be well placed to take on the additional but separate role of CDMC. However, this is a statutory appointment and the services to be provided need to be fully and precisely indicated. Any architect accepting such an appointment will need to understand fully the implications, be properly trained, and have appropriate indemnity cover. It is a function which could attract considerable liability in the event of injury to persons, or losses to clients should the works be delayed because of incidents or intervention by the Health and Safety Executive.

Architects should remember that even where a minor or domestic job is not notifiable to the Health and Safety Executive and there is no CDMC, the requirements on the designer under the CDM Regulations will still apply.

Appointment of architect as party wall surveyor

Under the RIBA Forms of Appointment the architect may undertake various duties in respect of party wall matters. These are described under *Architect's Guide to Job Administration: The Party Wall etc. Act 1996*. The need for a party wall surveyor will only arise in the event of a dispute with an adjoining owner. If the architect is to act as the party wall surveyor, this should always be via a separate appointment. The party wall surveyor is a statutory appointment and the duties are as described or implied by the Act. In particular, the surveyor must uphold the rights and obligations of both parties, rather than serve the interests of the client alone.

The RIBA Standard Forms of Appointment are not suitable without significant modification. In addition to the quasi-arbitral nature of the role, some of the Act's specific requirements would conflict with the standard terms of appointment. For example, under the Act the appointment cannot be rescinded by the building owner, whereas the RIBA forms provide for termination. It is therefore preferable for the appointment to be by a specially drafted letter or document.

PRE/SM4 RIBA Agreements

The RIBA publishes a comprehensive suite of Agreements which have been specifically designed to provide the components of a flexible system which can be assembled to create contracts tailored to the needs of individual projects. The system includes a wide range of Services Schedules to suit different situations.

The format of the RIBA Agreements 2007 is different from previous RIBA Standard Forms of Appointment to suit both paper and electronic usage. The full versatility of the new forms can be best appreciated in the online version, where you are able to customise the content of the components to suit the project in question. The full range of documents is listed below but for further information on the forms you are advised to go to www.ribabookshops.com/agreements

The full suite of RIBA Agreements are as follows, and these are available either electronically or in paper format:

- Standard Agreement for the appointment of an Architect (which replaces SFA/99 and CE/99)
- Standard Agreement for the appointment of a Consultant (which replaces PM/99, PS/99 and DB1/99)
- Concise Agreement for the appointment of an Architect (which replaces SW/99)
- Concise Agreement for the appointment of a Consultant
- Domestic Project Agreement for the appointment of an Architect (which replaces the Domestic Project Pack)
- Domestic Project Agreement for the appointment of a Consultant
- Agreement for the appointment of a Sub-Consultant (which replaces SC/99)
- Supplementary Schedule for a Contractor's Design Services (which replaces DB2/99)

The online service also provides schedules which are not available in paper and allow for greater flexibility in the use of the Agreements. The additional schedules available in PDF and RTF formats are used instead of or alongside the Role Specifications, Design Services Schedule or Services for a Small Project. They comprise:

- Schedule of Access Management Services
- Contractor's Design Services
- CDM Coordinator's Services
- Design Services for a Historic Building or Conservation Project
- Initial Occupation and Post-occupation Evaluation Services

- Schedule of Interior Design Services
- Master Planning Services
- Schedule of Multi-disciplinary Services
- Project Management Services

Draft Supplementary Agreements are also available:

- Sub-Consultant's Warranty
- Third Party Rights Schedule
- Consultant Switch or Novation

Client Guides in PDF format are also available to explain a particular service:

- Guide to Access Management Services
- Working with an Architect
- Working with an Architect: Repair and alteration of historic buildings
- Guide to Initial Occupation and Post-occupation Evaluation Services

Other appointments

Where specially drafted terms are being proposed these should always be checked against those in the standard forms. For small jobs the terms in C-Con-07 would form a useful checklist, otherwise legal advice may need to be sought. In all cases where non-standard terms are being proposed the architect should inform his or her insurers. For certain specific roles not covered above, the following forms may be useful:

- Adjudicator: the JCT publishes a form of appointment for an adjudicator (with a version for a named adjudicator) which must be used where an adjudicator is appointed in a dispute relating to a JCT form. The CIC model Adjudication Procedure includes an agreement on appointment of an adjudicator.
- Arbitrator: normally arbitrators set their own terms of appointment.
- Conciliator: the RIBA has a standard form for use with the RIBA Conciliation Procedure Party wall surveyor: this should be dealt with using a specially drafted letter or document. Guidance is set out in *Architect's Guide to Job Administration, the Party Wall etc. Act 1996*, which includes a letter of authorisation which must be obtained from the Appointing Owner before proceeding.
- Clerks of Works: the Institute of Clerks of Works publishes an appointment document.

Figures

Figure PRE1: Specimen letter to architect formerly engaged on project

IVOR B'ARCH Architects LLP

Prospect Drive, Thawbridge BS17 2ZX

T: 0100 012 023
F: 0100 012 024
E: mailto:ivor@b_arch.com

We understand that you were engaged by (the clients) to work on this project but that the arrangement has been properly terminated.

Under Rule 3.5 of the RIBA Code of Professional Conduct we are obliged to notify you that (the clients) have now appointed us as architects for this project.

We would be pleased to have your written confirmation that there are no matters outstanding which should be drawn to our attention at this stage.

Figure PRE2: Specimen project resource planning sheet

Job no: Job title:

Project resource planning sheet

Budget cost		Commencement				Completion				
		Estimated number of site visits								
Stage		A-B	C	D	E	F-G	H	J	K-L	
Start										
Finish										
Staff grade/name	£ per hour	Hours	Hours	Hours	Hours	Hours	Hours	Hours	Hours	Total
Ivor Barch partner	100	10	5							1,500
C. Smith architect	75	10	25	40	40	50			25	14,250
W. Blaggs technician	25	2	10	10	120	200				8,550
Stage total										
Expenses										
Total										

1. Estimate duration of Work Stages with start and finish entries.

2. List staff assigned to job, grade, unit rate and estimated hours under Work Stages. Rates should include for overheads, profit and reserves.

3. Enter estimated expenses likely to be incurred against headings such as car milage, travel fares, subsistence, etc.

Figure PRE3: Specimen letter confirming preliminary agreement

IVOR B'ARCH Architects LLP

Prospect Drive, Thawbridge BS17 2ZX

T: 0100 012 023
F: 0100 012 024
E: mailto:ivor@b_arch.com

We are writing about the terms of our appointment for this project.

You have asked us to undertake some preliminary services so that
the project may proceed, and we confirm these as follows:

_____

_____

It is understood that if you subsequently instruct us to undertake
other preliminary services, you will confirm this in writing. All these
services will be charged on a time basis at the following rates:

Principals	£ _____ per _____
Senior architectural staff	£ _____ per _____
Other architectural staff	£ _____ per _____
Administrative staff	£ _____ per _____

In addition, the following expenses will be charged:

_____

_____

Invoices will be submitted monthly. VAT is chargeable, where applicable,
at the current standard rate on all fees and expenses.

For the above services to be provided effectively, you will also need to appoint:

_____

_____

You should note that other financial commitments at this stage may include:

_____

_____

We will provide these services on the basis of the conditions included in the Form
of Agreement, a copy of which is enclosed [if appropriate at this stage].

We envisage that this preliminary appointment will continue for approximately
_____ months while we conclude the principal Agreement. When the principal
Agreement has been entered into, this appointment will be subsumed into
it, and fees invoiced under this letter will rank as payments on account.

Please confirm your acceptance of the appointment set out in this
letter by signing the enclosed copy and returning it to us.

PREPARATION > STAGES A-B

Appraisal and Design Brief

STAGE DESCRIPTION

Stage A: Appraisal, as defined in *RIBA Outline Plan of Work 2007*:

■ Identification of client's needs and objectives, business case and possible constraints on development. Preparation of feasibility studies and assessment of options to enable the client to decide whether to proceed

Stage B: Design Brief, as defined in *RIBA Outline Plan of Work 2007*:

■ Development of client's initial statement of requirements into the Design Brief by or on behalf of the client, confirming key requirements and constraints. Identification of procurement method, procedures, organisational structure and range of consultants and others to be engaged for the project

CONTENTS

CONTENTS (CONTINUED)

Stage Description

Stages A and B are often grouped for purposes of charging fees but, although there is much overlap, some distinction is possible, and they are separated in the Plan of Work.

The Plan of Work describes A: Appraisal as 'Identification of client's needs and objectives, business case and possible constraints on development. Preparation of feasibility studies and assessment of options to enable the client to decide whether to proceed.'

Stage A is therefore the stage when requirements are clarified and a strategy for action prepared. It is important at this stage to raise fundamental questions regarding the project, for example whether there is a need for a new building, or whether adaptation and reorganisation of the client's existing premises might not satisfy existing needs. Key issues such as funding, budget, project duration and building lifespan should be addressed. This stage may or may not involve outside consultants; with larger or more experienced clients the process of appraisal may be handled by the client body itself. The stage should culminate in a 'statement of need' which will form the basis of the Design Brief.

The Plan of Work describes Stage B: Design Brief as 'Development of client's initial statement of requirements into the Design Brief by or on behalf of the client, confirming key requirements and constraints. Identification of procurement method, procedures, organisational structure and range of consultants and others to be engaged for the project.'

Stage B includes such studies as may be relevant to determine what services will be necessary and whether it is feasible to achieve the project aims within the defined constraints. Such studies may be undertaken initially by the client organisation with in-house expertise or by a project manager or architect before the appointment of other consultants. Professional advisers may be commissioned solely for Stage B, more particularly in the case of major projects where demonstrable impartiality and objectivity are required by a client body. However, for the majority of commissions the architect as designer is well placed to undertake feasibility studies, advise on alternative design and constructional approaches, and identify what might be imposed by legislative and other constraints.

Stage B begins the process of team assembly. Although this will continue through C and the remaining stages, it is essential to have the composition of the complete team, and their various roles, agreed at an early stage and identified, whenever possible, in the appointment agreement. The Plan of Work can be used as a model to identify the services needed. The architect engaged as lead consultant would play a key role in this process. Alongside setting up the team, it is at this stage that partnering agreements may be finalised and project quality control systems put into place.

Stages A and B are present in all procurement routes. With design and build, the client must prepare a clear brief which may form part of, or evolve into, the Employer's Requirements under the design and build contract. The architect may be appointed by the client to assist in its preparation (e.g. DB/1), or (less common) if the contractor has been approached at an early stage, may be engaged by the contractor to assist in preparing feasibility proposals or studies for the client.

Under the Standard Conditions of Engagement (CA-S-07) the preparation of the Design Brief is the responsibility of the client and is 'received' by the architect at the start of Stage C, although the architect may contribute to its development through the preparation of studies, etc. If the architect is to be responsible for the preparation of this document, this must be identified in the terms of appointment as an 'Other Service'.

Terminology

The *RIBA Outline Plan of Work 2007* refers, under Preparation, to Stage A as Appraisal and Stage B as Design Brief.

The same terms are used in the Schedule of Design Services (SS-DS-07) and the Schedule of Contractor's Design Services (SS-CDE-07).

The Schedule of Services for a Small Project (SS-SP-07) refers to a combined Stage A-B – Preparation.

The Standard Conditions of Appointment (CA-S-07) define the Brief as:

The latest statement of requirements for the Project issued or approved by the client:

- *at inception, any initial statement by the client*
- *after clarification of the objectives, the Design Brief (or Output Specification)*
- *subsequently, any further development into the Project Brief*

Key Obligations

(from RIBA Agreements 2007: Standard Agreements (S-Con-07): Schedule of Design Services (SS-DS-07))

Stage A

Assist the client in defining the client's requirements.

Prepare feasibility studies to confirm the client's requirements.

Review with the client alternative project options.

Provide information for a report on cost implications.

Advise on the need for services by consultants and specialists.

Prepare and submit to the client a Stage A report.

Advise on methods of procuring construction.

Stage B

Contribute to preparation of the Design Brief, by or on behalf of the client, confirming key requirements and constraints and identifying procurement method, procedures, organisational structures, range of consultants and specialists to be engaged for the project.

A-B100   Preliminary Issues

A-B110   Information required

Check that all information necessary during Stage A-B is available, which might include the following:

- 'statement of need' to include the client's requirements, budget (A-B/CM1), project timetable and timetable for services

- information about the site and/or existing buildings to be supplied by the client. Legal aspects to be verified by the client

- further information from the client, e.g. accommodation schedule, manufacturing process, equipment, plant layout, safety policy, etc.

- information relating to the user client, e.g. location, security, particular needs, disabled access audits

- studies previously undertaken relevant to this project or site, e.g. social surveys, traffic or transport studies

- if available, Health and Safety File with information on site hazards or references to work carried out previously

- OS maps, site and/or building survey drawings

- documents referring to local history of site, political and social context, etc. (e.g. as found in library archives or press cuttings)

- environmental data, such as weather records, maps of the area, environmental studies, contaminated land investigations

- notes, sketches and photographs made during initial visits

- contributions, information and recommendations from consultant and specialists if they have not yet been appointed

NOTE *If procurement is through design and build for a contractor client:*

Employer's Requirements as issued to tenderers

A-B120	Appointment

ACTION A-B121	Establish scope, content and context for Stage A-B activities. Put it into context, particularly if material produced is likely to be acted upon by others taking over subsequent stages.

ACTION A-B122	Check appointing documents with respect to services and fees: • If the extent of professional services for Stage A-B is not yet settled, agree with the client and confirm in writing. • If the methods and levels of charging for Stage A-B are not yet settled, agree with the client and confirm in writing. • Because the project requirements, construction costs and architectural services are not fully defined at this stage, the fees for Stage A and B are often based on true costs rather than on a fixed sum or percentage fee.

ACTION A-B123	Establish, if possible, whether this is to be a continuing involvement for full services or likely to be a partial service confined to this Stage.

ACTION A-B124	Check with professional indemnity insurers whether the project seems likely to call for services outside those covered by the policy. For example, the architect might find it necessary to engage other consultants directly, or might be called upon to give advice on self-build operations, or might act as manager for a series of separate trades contracts. Cover could also be called into question because of the nature or scale of operations, or because of stipulations by the client as to the amount or duration of cover required. If the architect is to engage sub-consultants directly, check competence and resources, particularly with regard to CDM Regulations. Consider the use of CA-SC-07.

ACTION A-B125	Assess office resources needed for Stage A-B and ensure that they are available and adequate.	
ACTION A-B126	Review how in-house quality management procedures will be applied to the project. These may include the preparation of a project quality plan in an appropriate form. A project quality plan provides a mechanism to link the specific requirements of the project to an office quality-management system which might already exist. It will not necessarily mean the development of a new document or procedures over and above those that already exist. Refer to the RIBA QM Toolkit (see Further Reading).	SEE ALSO **A-B/SM7**

A-B130   Client

ACTION A-B131	Check the identity of the client's representative, project team/personnel/authorised agents. Check that the client has made organisational arrangements to deal with questions, supply information and take decisions. Under the Standard Conditions (CA-S-07) or a Letter of Appointment with the Concise Conditions (ML-C-07), the client's representative is to have authority to act.	
ACTION A-B132	Obtain from the client the project requirements, budget and timetable and any other project data being supplied by the client. Check these carefully, question incompatibilities and agree priorities.	SEE ALSO **A-B/SM1**
ACTION A-B133	Alert the client straight away to key issues that may be missing from these requirements and will need to be addressed in the client's Design Brief, for example strategy for disabled access, security policy and environmental policy.	SEE ALSO **A-B/SM2**

| ACTION A-B134 | Advise the client on the need to appoint a quantity surveyor (QS) and other consultants or specialists. Confirm who will make the appointments, the basis of agreements and the scope of such services. List the other consultants in the appointment agreement and any project quality plan. | SEE ALSO **A-B/SM3** |

NOTE

Be clear about the professional services needed. If other consultants and specialists are needed, be prepared to explain their roles and responsibilities. The Plan of Work may be a useful tool at this stage for mapping out the tasks that must be performed and identifying who will perform them, although it should be noted that it does not list all appointments that may be needed, such as party wall surveyor or access auditor.

Try to secure agreement that all professional appointments are on mutually interlocking agreements with similar, if not identical, contractual conditions. RIBA Agreements are available in architect and consultant versions with identical conditions, but services schedules may be required for some disciplines.

| ACTION A-B135 | Explain to the client the options for procurement, and note any matters which could affect the particular choice. |

| ACTION A-B136 | Check with the client whether tendering for the particular project is likely to be subject to legislative control. This could have an effect on procurement methods and procedures. |

ACTION A-B137	Advise the client on statutory and other legal obligations, including:	SEE ALSO **A-B/SM4** **A-B/SM5**

- the need for various approvals under national legislation concerned with planning and building, and the additional requirements of any local legislation or legislation for the particular building type which might apply

- the fees payable to the relevant authority at the time of these applications

- the obligations of a client under the CDM Regulations, and other A-B/M5 health and safety legislation, as appropriate

- the need to appoint a CDM coordinator, where the law requires this

- the duties of the client as building owner under the Party Wall Act including the possible need to appoint a party wall surveyor, and the rights of adjoining owners to appoint their own surveyors

- possible duties of the client under Part IIA of the Environmental Protection Act 1990, if the site may contain contaminated land

ACTION A-B138	Provide proof of competence to client (CDM 2007).

ACTION A-B139	Check whether any information provided by the client is confidential, and enquire whether the client wishes to ensure confidentiality for the project. If not, and publicity is sought, is this likely to involve wider consultation, e.g. presentations to a user client or local amenity bodies?

A-B150   Consultant team

ACTION A-B151	Establish or review project quality management procedures in concert with relevant procedures of all consultant team members.

ACTION A-B152	Confirm the consultant team composition and identify a lead consultant.
ACTION A-B153	Identify functional relationship to CDM coordinator and project manager (if appointed) and establish the authority of the lead consultant and design leader.
ACTION A-B154	Identify need for a 'team' project quality plan and agree format with client and consultant team.
ACTION A-B155	Check the scope of professional services agreed with other consultants as they are appointed.
ACTION A-B156	Confirm agreed policy of consultants and specialists concerning accountability, warranties, professional indemnity insurance, etc.
ACTION A-B157	Appraise client requirements and agree input to the stage by consultant team members.
ACTION A-B158	Confirm stage timetable for services and note its relationship to the project timetable as agreed with the client. The timetable should show critical points by which information from the client and consultant team members will be required.
ACTION A-B159	Establish arrangements for communication between client representative, CDM coordinator, project manager and consultant team leader.

ACTION A-B160	Agree working methods and procedures with the consultant team members, including:	SEE ALSO **AB/SM7**
	• means for integrating and coordinating effort and input	
	• compatibility in systems, software, etc.	
NOTE	*If the use of an extranet is proposed, review document management procedures for compatibility with Quality Assurance requirements. Consider the use of integrated Building Information Modeling together with the other consultant team members and the client.*	

ACTION A-B161	Establish programme and pattern for consultant team meetings.	SEE ALSO **Fig. A-B1**
	Fig. A-B1 is a specimen agenda for an initial consultant team meeting.	

ACTION A-B162	Establish regular report procedures to the client.	
NOTE	*Procedures for consultant team members should be clearly set out and closely followed throughout the project.*	

ACTION A-B163	Establish procedures for the client to 'sign off' the brief, design, etc. at relevant stages.	
NOTE	*Be strict about keeping to deadlines for reports and other submissions to the client.*	
	Set firm dates for approvals, instructions to proceed and the supply of information.	

A-B200   Stage Activities

A-B210   Developing the Design Brief

ACTION A-B211	Collate information from the QS, consultants and specialists.	

ACTION A-B212	Prepare feasibility studies and reports and submit to the client.	
NOTE	*The feasibility reports to the client will establish the basis upon which the project should proceed. It may be that the job is not feasible at all, or that the client's requirements, programme and cost limits cannot be reconciled. Make sure your reports are comprehensive, soundly researched and objective.*	

ACTION A-B213	Develop the client requirements into a Design Brief, or assist the client in developing its Design Brief.	SEE ALSO **A-B/SM2**

A-B230	Inspections/tests

ACTION A-B231	Obtain maps, studies and other contextual material.	
ACTION A-B232	Make an initial visit to the site and/or existing building.	SEE ALSO A-B/SM5 A-B/SM6
ACTION A-B233	Make a photographic record, notes and sketches as appropriate. File information and make an initial appraisal.	
ACTION A-B234	Advise the client about surveys needed and act as authorised. If independent surveyors are to do this, brief them fully. Refer to RIBA/ATS Survey Guidance.	
ACTION A-B235	Check for any reference in previous use or history of the site to contamination or the presence of hazardous substances, geological problems, underground services, etc.	

ACTION A-B236	Advise client, if appropriate, to authorise special surveys to investigate potential health and safety problems on presence of contaminated land.
NOTE	*It is important to identify at the earliest possible stage whether there are special conditions which will affect the viability of the project, e.g. contaminated land, asbestos in existing buildings, etc.*
	Inspect information provided by the client, including the Health and Safety File, if applicable.

ACTION A-B237	Obtain information on the existing and proposed mains services supplies.
ACTION A-B238	Obtain information on the existing and proposed traffic/ highways/access conditions.
ACTION A-B239	Establish whether an environmental impact study will be required.

A-B240	Consultations

ACTION A-B241	List authorities or bodies which may need to be contacted. Identify particular officers, names, addresses, phone numbers, etc.

ACTION A-B242	Review relevant legislation to identify potential constraints to development.

ACTION A-B243	Obtain access to the text of Acts, SIs and Approved Documents or Approved Codes of Practice, and study them carefully.

ACTION A-B244	Make a preliminary assessment of the necessary consents, applications and relevant procedures.
NOTE	*Check all information scrupulously; do not make assumptions. Consult the relevant authorities yourself and obtain or confirm their advice in writing.*

ACTION A-B245	Check the planning situation with the Planning Authority. For example:	SEE ALSO A-B/SM4

- whether there is any existing relevant permission, approval or consent still current – obtain the original notices if possible

- whether the proposed work requires planning permission, and if so which applications would be relevant

- whether there are special circumstances that need to be taken into account (e.g. Listed Building, Conservation Area, Enterprise Zone, Development Corporation, etc.)

- whether an environmental impact assessment will be expected, or might be helpful

- whether there is a known existence of hazardous substances or conditions due to earlier uses, likelihood of archaeological remains, etc.

- whether there are plans for compulsory purchase, or land take proposals for, say, road improvements which could affect use of the site

ACTION **A-B246**	Hold preliminary discussions with the planning officer to discuss key issues arising from the above checks. Establish the approach of the planning officer towards the principle of development as proposed and enquire if serious difficulties might be expected. Establish the measure of consultation which the planning officer would welcome or expect.
NOTE	*Consultation with statutory authorities is not included in S-Con-07 until Stage D, although it appears in Stage C in the Plan of Work. In practice, to establish feasibility of proposals, consultations are likely to be necessary at Stages A–C.*
ACTION **A-B247**	Check whether, particularly in the case of alterations to an existing building, the local authority Building Control department might be sympathetic to dispensations under Building Regulations.
ACTION **A-B248**	Check any concerns that the fire authority, police or military might have, particularly in an area of high sensitivity, and that might influence development or design.
ACTION **A-B249**	Check whether there are restrictions on site development potential due to mains or cables either below ground or overhead, and whether or not it is subject to easements or wayleaves.
ACTION **A-B250**	Check the position and capacity of mains drainage and services supplies from statutory undertakers.
NOTE	*Alert the client at a very early stage if it appears that there may be issues concerning the development which may require approval/ agreement of adjoining owners, e.g. whether rights of light, boundaries, rights of way such as for fire escapes or access will be affected. These will normally be dealt with by the client's solicitors but may take a considerable time to negotiate.*
ACTION **A-B251**	Check whether notices under the Party Wall etc. Act 1996 may be needed.
ACTION **A-B252**	Check whether third parties, e.g. landlord, estate surveyor, lessees, adjoining owners, etc. will need to be consulted. Initiate preliminary consultations if authorised by client.

| ACTION
A-B253 | Consult with user groups as authorised. | |
| NOTE | *Consultations with users or third parties do not form part of the Services under S-Con-07 unless identified under 'Other Services'.* | |

A-B260   Approvals/consents

| ACTION
A-B261 | Prepare an application to determine whether planning permission, conservation area consent or listed building consent is required, or whether there is need for an environmental impact assessment if appropriate. | SEE ALSO
AB/SM4 |

| ACTION
A-B262 | Prepare an application for outline planning permission, if appropriate. | |
| NOTE | *Applying for outline planning permission does not form part of the Services under S-Con-07 unless identified under 'Other Activities', so unless it is included in the appointment it will be necessary to obtain client authorisation.* | |

| ACTION
A-B263 | Prepare an application for certificates (e.g. Established Use) if appropriate. | |

| ACTION
A-B264 | Submit applications (if instructed by client) with relevant documents, including a cheque from the client for the appropriate fee. | |

A-B290   Cost planning

| ACTION
A-B291 | Together with other consultants, review the client budget figures and identify the sums included for actual construction work. | |

ACTION A-B292	Review the client requirements, programme and budget to assess compatibility. If not in balance, report to the client and seek clarification on priorities.
ACTION A-B293	Alert the client to the possible effects on the cost of the project due to inflation and the application of VAT.
ACTION A-B294	Review with other consultants possible sources of funding or grant aid and, if instructed, help to prepare a case or application. This might take the form of assistance from government departments, statutory bodies, local authorities, English Heritage or charitable trusts. Financial assistance is often subject to conditions which could affect design and specification proposals.

| ACTION A-B295 | Provide information for financial appraisal.

The report on cost implications should be structured under appropriate headings. It will normally be prepared by the quantity surveyor, if appointed. On jobs where there is no QS, cost estimates may need to be prepared by the architect – the appointment must make this clear. | SEE ALSO **A-B/SM8** |
|---|---|---|

A-B300   General Procedures

ACTION A-B301	Set up an in-house project team.
ACTION A-B302	Establish who will lead the office design unit. Identify personnel, roles, accountability and lines of communication and reporting within the office and with the external project team and client.
ACTION A-B303	Establish office administrative procedures.

ACTION A-B304	Open project files and allocate code letter or number to the project in accordance with office practice. Check with the client the full project title to be used. Refer to the RIBA QM Toolkit. Begin to compile a record of all key persons involved in the project, together with addresses, phone and fax numbers, etc. Check that names, titles or descriptions are correct, and check spelling. Circulate to all concerned.
ACTION A-B305	Set up procedures for regularly checking progress against the timetable for services, and for taking corrective action if necessary.
ACTION A-B306	Monitor office expenditure against fee income: • Set up office procedures for recording time spent on the project, by whom and the rates chargeable, and for noting expenses and disbursements incurred. • Set up procedures for regularly checking expenditure against the office job cost allocation.
ACTION A-B307	Arrange for regular reports to the client on fees and expenses incurred, and for accounts to be submitted at agreed intervals.
ACTION A-B308	Update project quality plan as appropriate.

A-B400   Stage Outputs

Tangible results/material produced before the conclusion of Stage A-B might include the following:

- a report to the client on studies to define the feasibility of the client's requirements. The report should analyse and appraise needs, give an environmental assessment and offer possible options, together with recommendations for the way forward – this might include conceptual drawings and diagrams

- a cost appraisal sufficiently detailed to enable a cost strategy to be devised

- where appropriate, a report on the condition of the fabric of an existing (perhaps historic) building, and suggestions for future uses

- where appropriate, proposals developed sufficiently to allow an application for outline planning permission

- Design Brief developed from the client requirements

NOTE   *If procurement is through design and build:*

- *for an employer client: initial suggestions for the Employer's Requirements.*

- *for a contractor client: a report to the client on Employer's Requirements as received, and related matters pending preparation of contractor's proposals.*

Supplementary Material

A-B/SM1: The briefing process

Compiling the brief and developing the design are activities which interact. Briefing is really a continuous process through to Detailed Proposals, but for convenience it can be regarded as evolving through three distinct phases. The client's 'statement of need' is the starting point, and it should never be forgotten that the client is at the core of the process. An inexperienced client, perhaps on a smaller size project, might welcome the assistance of the architect in preparing the statement of need.

The briefing process must be appropriate to the nature of the project. Some projects might depend upon planning and space standards which have already been widely researched and are generally available. Other projects might require considerable original investigation and extensive design studies. Such factors are likely to influence both the cost and duration of the design process, and the development of the brief.

The statement of need

The statement of need should set out the objectives which the client wishes to achieve in the project and will probably refer to functional requirements, environmental standards, levels of quality, lifespan and maintenance.

The statement may be anything from a broad preliminary statement of interest to a comprehensive set of technical requirements. It will rarely be sufficiently clear or detailed for design work but it should be seen as the basis for feasibility studies. The Brief should:

- state clearly the client's mission and objectives
- set out the client's needs
- indicate the impact of not meeting the needs
- identify the triggers for change
- place the client's needs in a historic context, e.g. a pattern of growth and change
- state what is expected in response to this statement
- state the sort of decisions needed and from whom

Considerable further investigation and development work will be necessary to bring it to the level of a Design Brief by the end of Stage A-B. However, it should be seen as an important part of developing the brief, and as such should be a formalised document to be agreed with the client.

The Design Brief

The Design Brief should be a document which covers the technical, managerial and design intentions, and shows how these requirements are to be met. It is likely to be the result of research and development involving all the consultant team, with additional expertise and advice from commissioned specialists. It will be the outcome of activities such as:

- feasibility studies
- site or building survey and studies
- research into functional needs
- accessibility audits
- environmental impact considerations
- statutory constraints
- cost appraisal studies

It should include:

- the mission statement
- the context
- organisational structure and function
- overall scope and purpose of the project
- programme, including phasing
- statements on size and capacity requirements and functions to be accommodated
- global capital expenditure budget and cash flow constraints
- targets and constraints on operating expenditure and other whole-life costs
- internal and external environmental requirements
- technology to be incorporated or accommodated, including equipment, services and IT
- quality requirements for design, materials, construction and long-term maintenance
- what is expected in response to the brief
- how the success of the project will be measured
- statutory requirements

A detailed checklist for the Design Brief is given in A-B/SM2.

The Design Brief should be seen as a starting point for the development of the Project Brief and should be formalised by the end of Stage A-B.

The Project Brief

The Project Brief should further define all design requirements. It should be prepared by the architect in collaboration with the client, and with coordinated contributions from all consultants and specialists, and the health and safety planning supervisor. Development of this Project Brief will probably require:

- assembly of all relevant information
- design studies and investigations
- preparation of detailed design proposals
- preparation of a cost plan

The Project Brief is the foundation on which the design will develop, and serves as a yardstick against which further design development can be measured. As such it is a factual record and a document of importance.

The Project Brief is the last stage in the briefing process and may be equated with the end of Plan of Work Stage D. It will evolve through Stages C and D, and an accurate record should be kept of the stage it reached at the end of Stage C. The Project Brief will be the basis for further detailed design work.

The CIB report

Briefing the Team states that it should cover:

- the aim of the design, including prioritised project objectives
- the site, including details of accessibility and planning
- the functions and activities of the client
- the structure of the client organisation
- the size and configuration of the facilities
- options for environmental delivery and control
- servicing options and specification implications, e.g. security, deliveries, access, workplace, etc.
- outline specifications of general and specific areas
- a budget for all elements
- the procurement process
- environmental policy, including energy
- the project execution plan
- key targets for quality, time and cost, including milestones for decisions
- a method for assessing and managing risks and validating design proposals

A detailed checklist for the Project Brief is given in D/SM2.

The Project Brief should be signed off by the client after approval. Any subsequent changes to the signed-off Project Brief should be recorded, identifying their impact on the project and architects' services, and formally agreed with the client.

The steps outlined above are likely to be found in most projects of reasonable substance or complexity.

The briefing process is something that should always be developed systematically. It provides the framework within which the design can be developed and it is an indispensable part of quality management. However, on projects of a more domestic scale the design and briefing processes may be compressed. Nevertheless, sufficient time should be allowed for this work to be done thoroughly, and architects should resist jumping to quick design solutions which might not meet the client's requirements.

The process of brief development is iterative, and it should be accepted that clients sometimes wish to modify their requirements even after approval of the Project Brief. Major changes could lead to the abandoning of design work already completed, or could at least have a significant effect upon cost, time and statutory consents. It is therefore essential to have an identifiable approved Project Brief to start with, and to have a procedure for Brief Change Control as part of the quality management plan. This will enable the client to be aware of the implications of changes to the Project Brief before final instructions are given.

A-B/SM2: Design Brief checklist

A Design Brief checklist relevant at the end of Stage A-B might include the following:

General

- the client's objectives, requirements and established priorities and criteria
- quality standards
- the client's environmental policy
- life expectancy of building and components
- user client considerations
- access requirements, including disabled access
- security requirements
- health and safety policy
- budgets for security, energy and maintenance including cleaning (i.e. costs in use)
- detailed functional requirements of direct client/user client
- site history, topography and geology
- preferred spatial relationships and orientation
- studies previously commissioned
- plans for future expansion
- exact location of boundaries
- other parties known to have expressed an interest, e.g. English Heritage, Royal Fine Arts Commission, etc.

Planning and building considerations

- known constraints arising from previous consents or conditions
- likelihood of planning gain or Section 106 Agreement
- impact of the local development plan
- leasehold/freehold interests and party walls, rights of light, access or other known easements

Environmental

- services below ground and known restrictions on development
- likely parking requirements
- likelihood of archaeological or antiquarian discoveries
- known road widening or development plans
- known problems with the site, e.g. geological conditions, hazardous substances, presence of contaminated land
- known problems with the buildings, e.g. presence of asbestos

Financial

- funding or institutional requirements or restrictions
- approximate cost per m² if speculative development
- grants, subsidies or information relating to tax advantages (e.g. VAT)

A-B/SM3: Consultant team appointments and working

Appointments

When acting as lead consultant, the architect should advise the client on the appointment of other consultants and specialists as necessary. The appointment and payment of consultants and specialists are matters best dealt with directly by the client; the services required should be identified in detail and recorded. The conditions of appointment for all consultants should be compatible and preferably to a common basis.

It is very important for the architect to know precisely what is included in the appointment terms of all consultants, so as to be able to minimise any overlap or duplication and to coordinate effectively the work of all the members of the consultant team. It is also desirable to ensure that all members are appointed under compatible conditions with a common policy concerning responsibilities, insurance, collateral agreements, etc.

The *RIBA Plan of Work: Multi-Disciplinary Services* serves as a useful table of the services that may need to be carried out, and could be referred to as the team is being appointed. It should be noted that, as explained in the Plan, not all of the services listed in the tables would be considered 'basic' or 'normal' by the relevant professional institution.

Depending on the nature and size of the project, a wide range of specialists and/or consultants may be needed at some stage. For example:

Surveyors:

- cost consultant
- land surveyor
- building surveyor
- party wall surveyor

Engineering consultants:

- civil engineer (including geotechnics)
- structural engineer

Building services consultants:

- heating and ventilating engineer
- electrical engineer
- lighting consultant

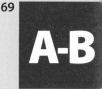

Other consultants and specialists:

- CDM coordinator
- landscape consultant
- acoustic consultant
- conservator
- health and safety consultant
- disabled access consultant
- fire engineering consultant
- public health consultant
- drainage consultant
- interior design consultant
- facilities management consultant
- security adviser

Of these, the appointments most likely to be relevant at Stage A-B are:

Cost consultants. Standard conditions of engagement are published by the Royal Institution of Chartered Surveyors (RICS) relating to a wide range of services. These need to be examined carefully to establish which services are to be provided for the particular appointment.

Structural engineers. Standard conditions of engagement and a number of different forms of agreement are published by the Association of Consulting Engineers (ACE). Normal services for structural work are arranged broadly in accordance with the Plan of Work stages. These need to be examined carefully to establish which services are to be provided for the particular appointment.

Building services engineers. Standard conditions of engagement are published by the Association of Consulting Engineers. The basic range of services can include Full Duties, Abridged Duties or Performance Duties. The conditions need to be examined carefully to establish which services are to be provided for the particular appointment.

With engineering services, architects are reminded that:

(a) 'working drawings' as understood in architectural terminology are not produced by mechanical and electrical (M&E) consultants

(b) 'builders work' drawings are for the architect to arrange, making sure that requirements for holes, shafts, access, insulation, etc. are properly coordinated and integrated into the design

(c) 'coordination drawings', where commissioned, should show detailed layouts and their relationship to plant rooms, spaces, structure, etc.

(d) 'installation drawings' (or 'shop drawings') are produced by the subcontractors or suppliers, and may be expected to show only general lines of pipework, fabrication and equipment installation details for comment by the engineering services consultant prior to fabrication or installation

It is normally the architect's responsibility to coordinate and integrate the work of consultants and specialists into the overall design. To this end, architects will need to inspect drawings submitted by specialists. However, contract documents should clearly place the responsibility for coordination of work being carried out on site with the main contractor.

Sub-consultants. If the architect is to appoint sub-consultants directly, great care must be taken to check their competence and resources with respect to Health and Safety Regulations and their PI insurance provisions. Reference can be made to Section 2 of Tim Jefferies' *A Model for a Quality Management System*. The RIBA Agreement for the Appointment of a Sub-Consultant (SubCon-07) should be used wherever possible.

Consultant team roles and responsibilities

Cost consultant. The cost consultant can assist the architect in assessing economic site use and advising on procurement methods. They can analyse cost information on other similar projects, local levels of building costs and cost trends, etc., and can judge whether the client's budget is realistic and compatible with other stated requirements.

The cost consultant should cooperate with the CDM coordinator, liaise with other consultants and specialists, attend consultant team meetings, and prepare the financial appraisal for the feasibility report.

Structural engineer. The structural engineer can advise the architect about local conditions relevant to the site, such as soil and geotechnical factors, roads, sewers, water supply, etc. They can:

- obtain existing information and interpret it
- identify hazards and hazardous substances
- arrange for site, structural and drainage surveys
- advise on alternative structural solutions
- prepare cost planning information for the QS
- prepare design criteria and calculations
- advise on structural aspects of party walls, temporary structures and demolition work

The structural engineer should cooperate with the CDM coordinator, liaise with other consultants and specialists, attend consultant team meetings and contribute to the feasibility report.

Building services engineers. The mechanical and electrical engineers should cooperate with the planning supervisor, and liaise with the architect and the structural engineer to study climatic conditions, energy use and conservation, emission problems, etc., and should consult relevant authorities as necessary.

The M&E engineers can:

- provide details of load and space requirements for services
- prepare feasibility studies, estimates, forecasts and maintenance cost options
- assist in dealings with statutory bodies
- prepare outline schemes
- prepare energy management studies and reports
- prepare design criteria and calculations
- advise on installation options and cost implications
- advise on energy, cost/benefit and running costs

They should attend consultant team meetings and contribute to the feasibility report.

Consultant team meetings

The consultant team will probably need to be enlarged during the development of the project. However, it is essential that it is formally constituted with a proper definition of responsibility and clearly accepted roles. Regular consultant team meetings are important to review progress and to record decisions. A specimen agenda for the initial consultant team meeting is shown as Fig. A-B1, and although the list of items will need modifying as the project progresses, the main headings should remain consistent throughout. In this way the history of each aspect of job administration will be automatically recorded and can be easily traced.

A system of regular reporting can be established. For example, the client's representative will report under the heading 'Brief', the architect under 'Site' and 'Approvals', the quantity surveyor under 'Cost control', and so on. The chair for these meetings is usually the lead consultant, or the architect acting as lead consultant.

A-B/SM4: Inspections, planning permission, other consents and approvals

Consents may have to be obtained during Stages A-B, C, D and F from authorities, organisations or persons having jurisdiction over, or rights affecting, the project, or who are affected by the project. Consents which could affect feasibility should be applied for during Stage A-B.

Depending on the nature of the project, the procurement method, the site and the amount of information available, each application for consent should be made at the earliest possible time in order to avoid abortive work.

Before initiating applications for consents:

Explain fully to the client what consents are necessary and what is likely to be involved.

- Discover whether the client has contacts or lines of communication with authorities or individuals concerned.
- Inform the client about fees payable directly by them.
- Inform the client about the likely timescale for processing applications and the degree of consultation.
- Make it clear to the client that architects do not obtain consents, this being beyond their power, but that they prepare submissions or make applications on behalf of their clients in accordance with the agreement for professional services.

Discover or confirm:

- the existing allocated or established use of the site
- whether the proposal is deemed to be 'development' under the Town and Country Planning Acts and so requiring planning permission
- the planning history of the site, noting important issues such as the dates and decisions of any earlier planning permissions for the site
- the effect on the site and the proposals of any policy statements or guidelines contained within the local development plan for the area
- whether the local authority has identified the site as containing contaminated land
- any likely limitations to the proposals or impositions on the developer through the use of Section 106 agreements or other planning conditions

Check relevant procedures

Check which of the following applications are relevant:

- for certificate of established use

- for mining or working of minerals
- for hazardous substances consent
- for outline planning permission
- for full planning permission to develop land
- for listed building consent
- for conservation area consent
- for approval of 'conditions' on a planning permission
- for varying or discharging conditions attached to listed building consent or conservation area consent
- for varying or revoking conditions attached to a planning permission
- for approval of reserved matters following an outline planning permission
- for a scheduled monument consent
- for a certificate of immunity from listing
- to fell or lop a tree
- to establish the need for an Environmental Impact Assessment
- to display signs and advertisements under the Control of Advertisement Regulations
- for notification under Circular 18/84 where the Crown is developing on Crown-owned land

The planning application

Make preparations:

- prepare all documentation on the assumption that it might serve as supporting evidence in an appeal
- confirm by letter all meetings, phone calls, etc. with the planning authority
- make sure that the client's representative also attends all critical meetings with the planning authority
- at an early stage consider project presentations to attract the interest and support of neighbourhood and parish groups, appropriate lobbies and news media

Check the following:

- dates and procedures of planning meetings
- probable date by which decision is to be given
- number and types of drawings required
- procedures, e.g. notices in the press, site notices, etc.
- processes for public consultation and response to any objections

When making a planning application, check that:

- forms are carefully completed – identify or list submitted drawings on forms or in covering letter
- an accurate site plan identifies the land concerned, clearly defined in red

- a covering letter accompanies the application, explaining features of the scheme
- an Ownership Certificate A (or B, C, D as appropriate) is served
- a cheque from the client for the appropriate sum is submitted at the same time (having checked the correct amount with the planning authority, as it usually increases year on year)
- the application is date-stamped by the planning authority (this defines the start of the period for determination)
- a copy of the written report by the planning officer to the planning committee is obtained
- if permitted and appropriate, oral representation is made to the planning committee

The planning meeting

If appropriate, attend critical meetings with the client's representative. Arrange for a shorthand note to be taken by another person. If planning permission is refused and an appeal is contemplated, send your account of proceedings to the chief executive of the authority. If not dissented from, it may have the status of 'agreed notes'. Examine the agenda and record of the meeting; these may constitute the basis for an appeal.

A-B/SM5: Health and safety checklists

Legislation

The principal legislation is the Health and Safety at Work etc. Act 1974, which sets out general duties on the part of both employers and employees. These were reinforced with the introduction of the Management of Health and Safety at Work Regulations 1992.

The Workplace (Health, Safety and Welfare) Regulations 1992 are relevant at Stage A-B. Although they place a duty on employers in respect of workplaces under their control, there are implications for the way in which new workplaces are designed and fitted out. This can be in respect of planning (e.g. traffic routes, escalators, room dimensions, sanitary provisions, etc.), finishes (e.g. floors, wall surfaces) and installations (e.g. lighting, heating, ventilation). The Regulations are concerned not only with the initial provision of safe conditions for staff but also with safety for cleaning and maintenance.

The RIBA provides guidance on safety for personnel visiting building sites (see Fig. A-B2) and this should be issued to staff and strictly observed.

The Construction (Design and Management) Regulations 2007 ('the CDM Regulations') implement an EC Directive which requires that account be taken of the general principles of prevention concerning health and safety during the stages of project design organisation, construction and future maintenance. The Regulations impose duties on the client, designer, CDM coordinator and principal contractor. They apply to nearly all projects where construction work will be of more than 30 days' duration or where more than 500 person days of construction work are involved, except in the case of domestic clients undertaking work on their own residences solely for their own occupation.

The architect's role

The architect, when acting as lead consultant or 'Designer' (as referred to in the CDM Regulations), should carefully study the text of the Regulations and the Approved Code of Practice. It would also be wise to check the following:

- that the client is aware of legal duty to appoint a CDM coordinator 'as soon as practicable', and a principal contractor – the client must be satisfied as to the competence and resources of both, concerning health and safety matters
- that the client is aware of legal duty to make available a Health and Safety File in respect of work previously carried out, and other relevant information concerning the site or premises
- that any sub-consultants employed directly by the architect have the necessary

competence and resources

- that inspections and surveys of site or buildings cover all matters which might indicate potential health and safety hazards – this is a Designer's duty, and if a detailed survey is thought necessary, the client must be prepared to pay for it
- that when undertaking risk assessments, proper consideration is given to eliminating or reducing potential health and safety hazards when planning site layouts or development – this will include the way that the contractor's operations on site are to be planned
- that there is full cooperation between the lead consultant and all others having a design input (including consultants and specialist subcontractors) with regard to health and safety matters
- that there is full cooperation with the planning supervisor over the production of information which may be relevant for the pre-tender Health and Safety Plan
- that the CDM coordinator is invited to attend consultant team meetings, and to comment as appropriate
- that in all design development the issues of safe specification, safe buildability and maintenance are kept fully in mind
- that the pre-tender Health and Safety Plan is part of the tender documentation supplied to the principal contractor and subcontractors
- that tenders are carefully examined to make sure that the selected principal contractor has the necessary competence and resources available to deal with health and safety matters, and that price and programme reflect this
- that the building contract has provisions for compliance with Health and Safety Regulations, and for the contractor to cooperate with the planning supervisor and provide 'as built' information, etc.
- that the client is aware that no work must start on site before a construction phase Health and Safety Plan has been produced by the principal contractor as a management document for the works
- that a copy of any architect's instruction or variation with health and safety implications is passed to the planning supervisor, and that the construction phase Health and Safety Plan can be updated accordingly
- that relevant information is passed to the CDM coordinator from time to time for possible inclusion in the Health and Safety File

The CDM coordinator

Where this function is discharged by the architect on smaller contracts, it should be seen as a separate appointment, made via a separate appointing document and with an identifiably separate fee.

Where an independent planning supervisor is to be appointed, an architect not otherwise involved in the job might be a suitable person. In all cases such appointments should only be considered by architects who have undergone proper training, fully understand the risks and have appropriate insurance cover.

Lead consultants or consultant team leaders working on a project where an independent planning supervisor has been appointed would do well to check that this appointee:

- gives proper notice to the Health and Safety Executive initially
- cooperates effectively in structuring information for a pre-tender Health and Safety Plan
- is thorough over the evaluation of health and safety aspects of the principal contractor's tenders, and is prepared to advise the client impartially
- is thorough but reasonable in evaluating the acceptability of the construction phase Health and Safety Plan from the principal contractor and as updated from time to time
- will prepare the statutory Health and Safety File for deposit with the client at the conclusion of construction, and will explain to the client their obligations concerning its safekeeping and future use

These may not be statutory duties but such checks are very much in the spirit of the legislation and certainly demonstrate the use of reasonable skill and care.

The Health and Safety Notice

This Notice, which is a statutory requirement, is normally submitted by the CDM coordinator to the Health and Safety Executive. It should include the particulars listed below, as they become known:

- date of forwarding
- address of construction site
- name and address of client
- type of project
- name and address of planning supervisor
- declaration confirming appointment of planning supervisor
- name and address of principal contractor
- declaration confirming appointment of principal contractor
- date for commencement of construction
- contract period for construction
- estimated maximum number of workforce
- total number of contractors (i.e. principal contractor and nominated/approved subcontractors) expected on site
- names and addresses of nominated/approved subcontractors already selected

The Health and Safety Plan

The Health and Safety Plan, a document for which the CDM coordinator should assume responsibility pre-tender, and for which the principal contractor is responsible, at construction phase might include:

- name of client
- nature of construction work and expected timetable
- existing environment (e.g. land uses, planning restrictions, services which might have health and safety implications, traffic systems and restrictions which might affect site working)
- ground conditions and possible hazards
- existing buildings: possible hazards, instability problems, special health problems associated with materials, etc.
- Health and Safety File particulars from previous works, supplied by client/ owner
- design principles (e.g. structural design precautions), risk hazards which are unavoidable, etc.
- construction information and choice of materials likely to cause health hazards and which cannot be avoided
- site access, egress, organisation of working
- particular precautions where exclusive possession is not available
- procedures for dealing with unforeseeable circumstances, and updates to the Health and Safety Plan

The Health and Safety File

The Health and Safety File, a document for which the CDM coordinator should assume responsibility, is to be deposited with the client at the completion of the contract. It will probably be assembled from information acquired gradually and steadily as the works progress. The client might need briefing as to its purpose, safekeeping and future use.

The File will be part record and part maintenance manual. It should include the following:

- design criteria
- general details of constructional systems and methods, materials used and any potentially hazardous aspects
- record drawings ('as built')
- details of equipment, finishes and maintenance facilities (e.g. window cleaning)
- maintenance procedures for the structure and finishes, including details and schedules by manufacturers and installers

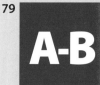

- operating instructions and maintenance manuals produced by consultants, subcontractors and suppliers for services installations, with recommendations for renewal and replacement cycle of plant and equipment
- information on location, setting and servicing of all services installations including alarms

A-B/SM6: Inspecting the site

Proper inspections and surveys of sites and existing buildings are essential at Stage A-B. Rough preliminary surveys are not good enough and are an inadequate basis on which to judge feasibility. Ill-founded recommendations at this stage can lead to serious problems later.

When considering survey action, try to establish:

* the kind of survey needed and precisely what is to be surveyed
* who will carry out the survey – the practice's own staff, external land or building surveyors, or other specialists
* who will pay for the survey and where liability will rest in the event of errors

Identify the boundaries of the site to be surveyed or the limits of the building. Confirm with the client that access will be available and obtain keys if necessary. Notify persons on site as appropriate.

Do not overlook statutory obligations arising, particularly those concerning occupiers' liability, and health and safety. Always heed the RIBA Safety Code for occupied building sites and unoccupied buildings and sites (see Fig. A-B2).

Information about immediate area

Check:

* general context and character, outstanding visual features
* local development plan, action area plans, construction work currently under way
* evidence of social and economic patterns
* traffic movement patterns, noise, pollution
* derelict areas, nearby black spots, visually detracting features

Visual inspection of site

Check:

* aspect, orientation, shelter, overshadowing from adjacent buildings or trees
* hedges, ditches, ponds, wet/soft patches, underground streams
* benchmarks, contours and slope of site
* paths, gates, stiles which might indicate rights of way
* overhead cables, pylons and poles
* possible health and safety hazards, e.g. flooding, exposure, unsafe trees, etc.
* properties adjoining the site, their condition, usage, evidence of subsidence, fire risks, party walls, etc.

A-B

- possible health and safety hazards such as radon or other gases, pollutants and contamination from previous use, filled basements, etc.
- adjacent waterways, railways, busy roads
- possible restrictions on site access, delivery or site working
- possible restrictions due to sensitive building uses adjacent, e.g. hospital, nursery school, law court

Site survey information

Refer to the RIBA/ATS Survey Guidance checklist.

If the site survey is to be undertaken by a surveying firm, make sure that this is agreed with the client as not being a part of the architect's services, and is to be paid for directly.

Confirm:

- by whom the surveyors are to be engaged
- how the surveying fees are to be paid
- who is doing which part of the work
- how the results are to be presented
- arrangements for access, security, protection and insurance

If appropriate, arrange for a survey of tree species and condition, and an analysis of topsoil.

The information presented in the survey plans and reports might be expected to include the following:

Plans, showing:

- existing and proposed boundaries
- outline of existing buildings and roads
- boundary fences, access ways, garden and adjacent walls, their height, profile, material, ownership and condition
- ditches, ponds, waterways above or below ground
- wet or bad patches (discover seasonal variations from local sources)
- rock outcrops and other geological features, their type and size
- position of trial holes
- rights of way/access (check with client's solicitors, local authority)

Sections, drawn on separate sheets, taken along the full length of section lines on the key drawings, to the same scale as the plan.

Levels, showing:

- position and level of benchmarks or basis of datum

- calculated levels in true relationship to an ordnance datum level
- spot levels on a 10 m grid related to ordnance survey grid, or closer where local variations occur, e.g. at changes of level, hillocks, etc.

Spot levels, indicating:

- the base of all trees
- all services covers, etc.
- pavement kerbs and road crowns where they enter the site

Indicate contours, intervals (in metres) and position of section lines (on grid lines where possible).

Indicate all services above and below ground adjacent to, connecting into or crossing the site with relevant levels, falls, heights, access points, manholes (show cover levels and inverts). Also:

- pylons, posts (show headroom)
- soil and surface water drains
- water mains
- electricity cables
- telecommunication cables
- gas mains
- any other services

Indicate trees, hedges and large shrubs, their height and position, spread of branches and diameter of trunk 1 m above ground level.

Soil investigations

On a domestic project or one which involves a relatively small and light structure, it might well be sufficient for the architect to instruct the digging of trial pits. These should be set out with regard to the siting of the proposed building. On anything larger, investigation by boreholes may be necessary to obtain information and data for the design and construction of foundations, underground structures, roadworks, earthworks, etc. On sites containing contaminated land or unstable landfill, specialist advice will be needed as to the surveying techniques to be used.

The structural engineer may be able to give preliminary advice by examining available information about the geology and history of the site, e.g. maps and memos produced by the Institute of Geological Sciences, Ordnance Survey maps, engineering data from earlier works in the area or aerial photographs.

The engineer should recommend the type and extent of investigations to be carried out, including the number of trial holes necessary to obtain an accurate assessment of the subsoil and water table conditions.

The investigating firm must allow for carrying out the work in accordance with any special requirements of the existing owners or occupiers of the site. They and/or their subcontractor specialists should be made responsible for all security, protection and related insurance during execution of the work.

The field work should be supervised by the engineer, and daily liaison should be maintained so that any variations indicated by the borehole findings can be made. Daily site records of boreholes should be sent to the engineer stating:

• borehole numbers and location
• date and times of boring
• type of plant and method of boring
• diameter of boring casing and core
• description of strata and depth of base of each stratum
• level at bottom of casing when sample taken, or in situ test carried out on each core drilled
• depths at which each sample was taken and in situ tests made
• water levels

On completing the site work, the contractor should submit to the engineer preliminary borehole logs together with a list of samples so that instructions can be given for laboratory testing.

The final site investigation should be submitted as a draft (for approval of its form, not its content). Unless otherwise specified it should contain:

• description of work carried out (i.e. site and laboratory work)
• borehole logs
• laboratory test results, including geological classification, index properties, acidity, sulphate content, etc.
• records of water levels in standpipes and/or piezometers installed in boreholes, with notes of any variations
• results of strength tests
• diagrammatic cross-section through site showing trial holes related to a datum and assumed connecting geological structure, water table, etc.
• plan showing position of trial holes, incorporated with main survey plan if appropriate

Surveys of existing buildings

It is essential that the architect personally walks through every room in the building to be surveyed, regardless of whether the survey is being done by in-house personnel or by a surveying firm. It is important to perceive the architectural character of a building and the way it has been constructed.

The measured survey drawings might show:

- plans, sections, elevations
- elevational features, e.g. plinths, string courses, openings
- precise levels at floors, datum, thickness and construction
- levels of external ground
- details of decoration, profiles, false columns, etc.
- finishes and colours
- loose equipment, landlord's fittings, etc.

A written report might include information that cannot be shown graphically, such as:

- structural and other defects and their causes
- dry rot, damp penetration, condensation
- infestation by rodents, beetles and other insects
- recent repairs and decoration
- settlement cracks, misshapen openings, gaps at skirtings and windows
- walls that are misaligned or have bulges
- sagging roofs, defective roof coverings
- deflection of beams or lintels, cracks at beam bearings

The architects/surveyors should state whether or not they were able to see inside the structure of the building and how much they were able to see. It is important not to infer the state of the whole building from sight of one part of it. A statement on the following lines should appear at the end of the relevant part of the report (as stipulated in most professional indemnity insurance policies):

> *It has not been possible to make a detailed examination of the floor or roof construction except at the positions described because material damage would have been caused in gaining access. It is therefore impossible to make any statement about the condition of the unexamined structure.*

Where appropriate, the client should be advised to call in specialists, e.g. mechanical, electrical, timber treatment, and should be asked for instructions regarding any fees, expenses and inconvenience arising from their investigations.

A-B/SM7: A project quality plan

References in this *Architect's Job Book* to setting up and developing a project quality plan are made against the background of the Standard for Quality Systems BS EN ISO 9001:1994. Quality management is concerned with consistent performance to stated requirements, and the system is essentially one of control. Likewise, the project quality plan document should be seen as the principal instrument for control and communication on the project. Reference should be made to the RIBA QM Toolkit.

Having an operational QM system is now a requirement for RIBA Chartered Practices. At the time of writing, a number of architects' practices have achieved certification status, and these will already be operating a system which includes project quality plans. Such a system is set out in the RIBA QM Toolkit and Jefferies (1999) *A Model for a Quality Management System*.

In addition to those who have formed third-party certification, many other practices also have systematic procedures – whether or not they describe these as 'quality management' – which constitute an effective framework for running the office and the individual jobs. There will probably be an office handbook or manual where the procedural framework is clearly set out. In addition to the office organisation, policy and review mechanism, the manual will probably describe general administrative procedures, the way appointments are to be formalised, job costing and fees, employing consultants, dealing with correspondence, management of design, producing and issuing drawings, administering contracts, and keeping records. These and other matters are all part of the way a methodical practice carries on its business.

Accordingly, where a formalised quality system does not exist, a project quality plan can still be created either as a stand-alone document or as part of a coordinated package making reference to other controlling documents or procedures. This may be provided in hard copy as well as software, written or diagrammatic. Many of the procedures might be described in detail elsewhere (e.g. in the office manual, handbook or other documents, such as this *Architect's Job Book*) and could be included by reference. Two alternative detailed and helpful project quality plans are set out in *A Model for a Quality Management System*. What follows is an outline of what a project quality plan might contain.

Project description

- the client's design requirements
- a synopsis of brief and priorities
- an intended lifespan of building overall, and of components
- constraints which arise from legislation or other sources

Project organisation

- the identity of the client and representatives
- an identified practice/project quality manager
- agreed procedures for consultations/approvals
- principal practice staff assigned to the project and their defined responsibilities
- project timetable/programmes

Consultant team

- consultants/specialists with design or other input
- defined responsibilities, including review procedures
- management, procedures for administration, including coordination

Control procedures

- brief development control and reviews
- design input control, design management and development, and patterns of design review
- design and information output control
- project specification basis and development
- project administration and document control procedures including roles associated with project extranets and Building Information Modeling systems
- procurement, and procedures for appointment of the project construction team
- contract administration procedures
- monitoring of contractors' quality management

Change control

- agreed procedures for modifications or changes to approved brief
- agreed procedures for modifications or changes to approved designs
- records of modifications or changes
- identification of documents subjected to revision, and withdrawal to prevent unintended use

Tests

- programme for inspections and tests, and personnel involved
- procedures and check sheets or reports to be used
- corrective action in the event of non-conforming work
- programme for audits, personnel involved and audit reports

Particular instructions

- those items in the practice's quality system to be expressly excluded in the case of this particular project
- items not covered by the practice's quality system to be specifically included in the case of this particular project

Records

- end of project reviews
- experience feedback studies and reports
- maintenance manuals and operating instructions
- as built information
- job records and files

To summarise, a project quality plan will be in the form most appropriate for the particular project. It should be a document which:

- defines activities and how they are to be carried out
- should be adequate for submission to a client for acceptance and review
- is reviewed regularly through the progress of the project, with amendments and revisions, as necessary, submitted for acceptance before implementation

A-B/SM8: Financial appraisal

The financial appraisal is usually prepared by the quantity surveyor. The QS is the expert on costs, and can call on a Royal Institute of Chartered Surveyors (RICS) or other information service, as well as their own knowledge and expertise. Such an appraisal could be a document to be developed as the design progresses, and form a basis for effective cost planning.

However, on a small project where no QS is appointed the architect may have to write an appraisal for inclusion in the feasibility report. This is likely to be little more than an estimate to test the viability of the client's budget figure. A proper cost plan will need to be developed later.

Where the architect undertakes to prepare this appraisal, the approach should be as follows.

Define status

Define the status of the appraisal, and set out the assumptions on which estimates are made. List any items of important information which were not available, and which items have not been included.

State basis for estimates

State the basis for estimates (e.g. cost indices, £m^2 etc.) on current or predicted rates (if projected, to what date).

Estimate capital cost

When estimating the capital cost of the building project, consider:

- location (e.g. whether remote) and access (e.g. a difficult, tight site)
- site investigation and abnormal site works
- demolition or preliminary contracts for enabling works
- programme and phasing
- building substructure and superstructure (e.g. systems, cladding, etc.)
- finishes (e.g. expensive or standard)
- engineering services installations
- designers' and contractors' contingencies
- fitting out and furnishings
- landscape treatment – both hard and soft, including planting

Other costs

Other costs to be taken into account might include:

- fees for statutory approvals
- fees and expenses for the consultant team
- fees and expenses for the planning supervisor

An estimate should also clarify the VAT position and the possible effects of inflation, and warn that fluctuations are possible after the start of the building contract, even a lump sum contract. It might also be helpful to suggest the phasing of payments so that the client can begin to consider how best to manage cash flow.

In addition to the estimate of the capital cost of the building project, the client will need to take into account the cost of the site, legal and other fees, finance costs, the risk and profit element, and an assessment of costs in use for the building.

Figures

Figure A-B1: Specimen agenda for initial consultant team meeting

Job no: Job title:

Agenda

1. Consultant team and reports

   Appointments, personnel
   Roles and responsibilities
   Lines of communication for policy/day-to-day matters
   Pattern and reporting procedures for future meetings
   Project programme
   Team members' programmes and progress

2. Brief

   Client's requirements
   Development of brief
   Changes to brief, implications and control procedures
   Pattern and procedures for reporting to client
   Preparation of Stage reports to client

3. Site

   Information from client about site, foreseeable hazards
   Assessment of risks
   Development constraints, physical and statutory
   Surveys and consents

4. Approvals

   Private individuals/bodies
   Funders, insurers
   Town and country planning
   Building Regulations
   Fire officer
   Legal (e.g. adjoining owners)

5. Health and safety

   Risk assessment
   Health and Safety File
   Health and Safety Plan

6. Design and cost control

   - Concepts
   - feasibility assessment
   - development of the Brief

   Coordination of design team effort

   - general design
   - structures
   - services

   Drawings

   - agreed methods, scales, software, referencing
   - cost control
   - development of cost plan
   - variations

7. Contract

   Priorities and phasing
   Programming
   Procurement
   Tendering procedures and documents,
   Health and Safety Plan

   - main contract
   - subcontracts

8. Any other business

9. Date of next meeting

Figure A-B2: RIBA Safety Code: visits to sites and unoccupied buildings

Health and Safety

Health and Safety legislation lays clear obligations on clients, designers, and principal contractors. The following code is complementary advice to all architects engaged in visits to buildings and sites.

Visits to building sites, unoccupied buildings and construction operations can be potentially dangerous. Consider the likely hazards. Follow the safety code.

1 Occupied building sites

The Contractor or occupier has a responsibility for the safety of persons lawfully on site. Do not enter sites or buildings without permission, and immediately report to the person in charge. Comply with all requests from the contractor, his representative or other supervisory staff. See the contractor when you arrive, and when you leave the site.

Wear suitable clothing, in particular protective headgear (a hard hat) and stout shoes or boots. Do not wear thin-soled or slippery shoes. Avoid loose clothes which might catch on an obstruction.

Check that ladders are securely fixed and that planks are secure. Beware of overhead projections, scaffolding and plant, and proceed with caution. Particular care is necessary in windy, cold, wet or muddy conditions. Keep clear of excavations and beware of openings in floors etc. Do not lean on guard rails, scaffoldings etc. Do not interfere with any temporary barriers, guard rails or lights. Beware of ladders on which the rungs may have rusted or rotted, and never climb a ladder which is not securely fixed at the top.

Do not touch any plant or equipment. Keep clear of machinery and stacked materials. Watch out for temporary cables, pumps, hoses and electric fittings.

Do not walk and look around at the same time. Keep one hand free at all times when moving. Make sure that you are in a safe and balanced position whenever making notes or taking photographs.

Report to the contractor anything that comes to your notice on the site as being unsafe.

2 Unoccupied buildings and sites

As a general rule do not visit an empty building or unoccupied site on your own. Make sure someone knows where you are, and at what time you expect to return.

Do not take chances. Do not visit an empty building if you think it unsafe. Do not visit an unoccupied site if you think it dangerous. Anticipate hazards.

Common dangers include:

– the possibility of partial or total structural collapse
– rotten or insecure floors and stairs
– hidden pits, ducts, openings etc, fragile construction, eg asbestos or plastic sheets on roofs
– space which has not been used or ventilated for some time
– live services
– contamination by chemicals or asbestos
– intruders who may still be around
– contamination by vermin or birds, or poisonous substances put down to control them.

Plan the visit and make sure that you take with you appropriate equipment and protective clothing. Apart from stout shoes and a hard hat, remember that unoccupied buildings can be dirty, damp, cold and dark; so go prepared.

Look for defects in the floors ahead, eg wet areas, holes, materials that might be covering up holes.

Familiarise yourself beforehand with the plan of the building, particularly the exit routes. Make sure that security devices on exits will allow you to reach safety quickly.

Walk over the structural members (eg joists, beams, etc) whenever possible - do not rely on floorboards alone.

Do not walk and look around at the same time. Keep one hand free at all times when moving. Do not walk and try to take notes at the same time. Make sure that you are in a safe and balanced position when taking photographs or stretching out to take measurements.

Check on protection when approaching stairwells, lift shafts, roof perimeters, etc.

Do not assume that services (eg cables, sockets, pipes, etc) are safe or have been isolated.

If you suspect the presence of gas, inflammable liquids, dangerous chemicals or free asbestos fibre leave the building immediately.

If you sustain cuts, penetration by nails or other serious injury, seek immediate medical advice.

Always heed these three golden rules:

– do not rush
– if uncertain do not proceed – seek advice or assistance
– do not smoke or use naked flame.

Concept

STAGE DESCRIPTION

As defined in *RIBA Outline Plan of Work 2007*:

- Implementation of Design Brief and input into Project Brief
- Preparation of Concept Design including outline proposals for structural and building services systems, outline specification and preliminary cost plan
- Review of procurement route

CONTENTS

Stage Description

This Stage starts with the receipt or sign off from the client of the Design Brief. The Design Brief may include details of any preferred option or feasibility study developed at Stage A-B which may form the basis for the outline proposals at Stage C.

 The Design Brief is now the basis for the architect's services which, if different from the services, cost or time targets in the agreement with the client, may require a formal variation by letter or deed.

With a traditional procurement method, during Stage C a design concept based on the Design Brief will usually be prepared. This will show the design analysis and options considered, and will be sufficiently detailed to establish in broad terms the outline proposal preferred. Presentation will normally entail drawings and a report, although more sophisticated techniques such as digital modelling may be employed where appropriate.

NOTE *Where no outline design concept is required – for example when conserving a historic building – Stage C will involve the presentation of Concept Designs appropriate to the commission.*

In parallel with the development of the design, the Design Brief will be evaluated and developed to form the Project Brief, a document which is finalised by the end of Stage D.

NOTE *Where the architect is appointed under the RIBA Concise Agreement (C–Con–07), Stages C and D are combined and preparation of the Project Brief is not defined, although a record of any changes made to the original brief may be appropriate.*

With design and build, where the architect is engaged by the employer for Stage C, a Concept Design may be developed to form part of the Employer's Requirements. The design will be taken to an extent related to the intended design contribution by the contractor.

With a contractor client, the employer's Design Brief may form a component part of the Requirements, and the architect will be involved in developing the contractor's proposals as a response to these Requirements. Tendering is often a two-stage process, and this might initially require a Concept Design only, with design development left until a later stage.

Key Obligations

(from RIBA Agreements 2007: Standard Agreements (S-Con-07): Schedule of Design Services (SS-DS-07))

Receive Design Brief; assist in the preparation of additional briefing data (Project Brief).

Prepare Concept Design, also showing Outline Proposals for structural and building services systems, and including outline specifications.

Review procurement method.

Provide information for approximate estimate of relevant cost.

Prepare and submit to client a Stage C report.

C100   Preliminary Issues

C110   Information required

Check that all information necessary during Stage C is available, which might include the following:

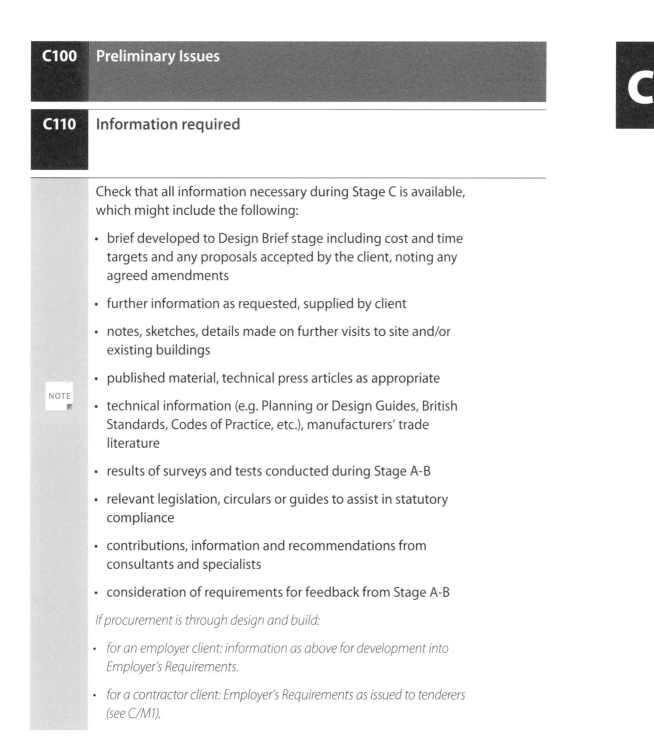

- brief developed to Design Brief stage including cost and time targets and any proposals accepted by the client, noting any agreed amendments

- further information as requested, supplied by client

- notes, sketches, details made on further visits to site and/or existing buildings

- published material, technical press articles as appropriate

- technical information (e.g. Planning or Design Guides, British Standards, Codes of Practice, etc.), manufacturers' trade literature

- results of surveys and tests conducted during Stage A-B

- relevant legislation, circulars or guides to assist in statutory compliance

- contributions, information and recommendations from consultants and specialists

- consideration of requirements for feedback from Stage A-B

If procurement is through design and build:

- *for an employer client: information as above for development into Employer's Requirements.*

- *for a contractor client: Employer's Requirements as issued to tenderers (see C/M1).*

NOTE

C120	Appointment

ACTION C121	Establish scope, content and context for Stage C activities. Put it into context particularly if previous stages undertaken by others, or material produced is likely to be acted upon by others taking over subsequent Stages.
ACTION C122	If coming new to the project at this Stage in the Plan of Work: • Ascertain that relevant Pre-Agreement and earlier Stage checks have been carried out. • Allow for familiarisation and reviewing of all usable material when agreeing fees and timetable with the client; confirm the role of the architect in relation to the rest of the consultant team if appointed, i.e. whether appointed as lead consultant, design leader or member, or whether a project manager has been appointed. Direct access to the client, particularly at design stages, is highly desirable. • Ensure that you have adequate professional indemnity insurance cover in accordance with ARB and RIBA requirements.
ACTION C123	Check that the client's instruction to proceed has been given and confirmed in writing.
ACTION C124	Check that client has signed off or approved the design brief.
ACTION C125	Check that client has settled all accounts to date.

ACTION **C126**	Check appointing documents with respect to services and fees.
	• If the services, cost or time targets are different from the agreement with the client, agree a formal variation by letter or deed as appropriate. Fees based on percentage of anticipated building costs or lump sum may have to be reassessed and agreed based on the updated Design Brief budget.
NOTE	• If the extent of professional services for Stage C is not settled, agree with the client and confirm in writing. If the methods and levels of charging for Stage C are not settled, agree with the client and confirm in writing.
	Enquire whether additional services will be wanted which are not included under the Agreement. These might extend to special studies, community surveys and participation exercises with a user client, attendance at meetings, presentation materials, etc.

ACTION **C127**	Assess office resources needed for Stage C and ensure that they are available and adequate.

ACTION **C128**	Carry out checks for compliance with in-house quality management procedures, including updated project quality plan.

ACTION **C129**	Review application of practice procedures to project.

C130　Client

ACTION **C131**	Alert the client to any matters raised during preliminary discussions with statutory or other bodies which seem likely to affect the brief or design proposals.

ACTION **C132**	Advise the client on the need to appoint further consultants and specialists. Decisions may be needed for Outline Proposals which require specialist advice on structure, services, and environmental and other matters.

ACTION C133	Advise the client on health and safety matters. Remind the client about the need to appoint or retain a CDM coordinator to coordinate matters connected with the pre-tender Health and Safety Plan at this design stage.
ACTION C134	Make specific requests to the client for further necessary information if that provided is not adequate.
ACTION C135	Review with the client the options for procurement and note any matters which could affect the particular choice. In particular it is important to identify at an early stage who will be carrying out all specialist areas of design, for example whether they will be handled by the consultant team or by specialist subcontractors. This has implications for the consultant's terms of appointment, liability and warranty arrangements as well as affecting the procurement route to be adopted.

NOTE *If procurement is through design and build:*

- *for an employer client, confirm with the client the extent of information to be included in the Employer's Requirements.*

- *for a contractor client, check the Employer's Requirements issued for tendering purposes, and advise the client on any apparent omissions or inconsistencies. Confirm with the client the extent of information to be provided for inclusion in the contractor's proposals.*

C150 Consultant team

ACTION C151	Establish or review project quality management procedures in concert with relevant procedures of all consultant team members.
ACTION C152	Check scope of professional services agreed with other consultants as they are appointed.

C

ACTION C153	Agree input to the Stage by consultant team members. Remind consultant team members contributing at Stage C to identify current legislation (e.g. Building Regulations, health and safety) with which the project must conform. Discuss with consultant team members the performance standards, environmental provisions and budget allocation required to comply with the brief, and the presentation of material in a way which can be readily integrated into the overall design concept.
ACTION C154	Confirm Stage timetable for services and note its relationship to the project timetable as agreed with the client. The timetable should show critical points by which information from the client and consultant team members will be required.
ACTION C155	Confirm arrangements for communication between client, planning supervisor, project manager and design leader.
ACTION C156	Cooperate with the planning supervisor and all other designers over carrying out risk assessments and in drafting the pre-tender Health and Safety Plan.
ACTION C157	Confirm programme and pattern for consultant team meetings.

C200 Stage Activities

C210 Developing the Project Brief and Concept Design

ACTION C211 (CONTINUES)	On receipt of the Design Brief, evaluate its content to establish that: • the client's stated objectives are reflected • an adequate basis for design is provided • the time and cost parameters are reasonable

ACTION C211 CONTINUED	• all the information the client should provide before design commences is provided
NOTE	*If changes to the brief are necessary, make sure that these are subject to the change control procedures established, for example in the project quality plan.*

ACTION C212	Advise the client of the results of the evaluation and seek instructions regarding any further information needed.

ACTION C213	If the Design Brief varies from any submissions to the client during Stages A or B consider what action may be required.

ACTION C214	Obtain relevant technical and trade literature.

ACTION C215	Obtain project-specific information from potential subcontractors and suppliers.

ACTION C216	Coordinate and integrate information from QS, other consultants and specialists.

ACTION C217	Commence development of Design Brief into Project Brief.

ACTION C218	Undertake design review as appropriate.

ACTION C219	Concept Design Proposals.
NOTE	*Innovation in design, specification or selection of materials and methods can involve risk. Take care that risks are assessed before proposals are finalised. Check and test against known criteria – do not trust to luck.*

ACTION C220	Prepare report and submit to the client.

C230 Inspections/tests

ACTION C231
Make further visits to the site and/or existing buildings as authorised.

ACTION C232
Carry out a visual inspection of the extent of existing buildings, site boundaries, etc. before completing outline design or proposals. If necessary, ask the client to ascertain the exact details of site boundaries, covenants, easements, etc. In the case of design and build particularly, the employer may carry total responsibility for accuracy.

ACTION C233
Carry out or supervise further survey work if appropriate and if instructed by the client.

ACTION C234
If appropriate, construct contour or block models or 3D CAD model to demonstrate options in Concept Design.

Consider need for tests using physical or computer models (e.g. in research laboratory using a wind tunnel, heliodon, artificial sky, etc.) to obtain and analyse information about environmental performance, air circulation, temperature distribution, etc.

ACTION C235
Prepare models for testing, and record and analyse results if instructed by client.

NOTE
Surveys, inspections or specialist investigations and preparation of special models do not form part of the Services under S-Con-07 unless identified under 'Other Services'.

C240 Consultations

ACTION C241
Hold informal discussions with authorities as appropriate before making formal submission for permission, approval or consent.

NOTE
Consultation with statutory authorities is not included in S-Con-07 until Stage D, although it appears in Stage C in the Plan of Work. In practice, to establish feasibility of proposals, consultations are likely to be necessary at Stages A–C.

ACTION **C242**	Hold discussions as appropriate with the planning officer.
ACTION **C243**	Discuss with the client the potential benefits in obtaining outline planning approval.
ACTION **C244**	Establish with the local authority building control department: • whether the project is one which will require approval under Building Regulations and, if so, whether this should be Building Notice or Full Plans submission • whether it would be more beneficial to submit Building Regulations applications to the local authority or an approved inspector, and report to the client • whether a dispensation would be likely where the legal requirements of Building Regulations could be particularly onerous and damaging to the architectural integrity of a historic building
ACTION **C245**	Check whether there is any local legislation, or legislation particular to the proposed development or building type, which should be complied with.
ACTION **C246** NOTE	Discuss with the relevant authorities the most satisfactory way of making provision for persons with a disability who could be expected to use the building. *It is important to advise the client about the current and future implications of the Disability Discrimination Act 1995. Even though not all sections are yet in force, it is important to avoid the client being placed in a position where work may need to be altered in the near future.*
ACTION **C247**	Check whether bodies such as the National Rivers Authority, British Waterways Board, etc. could have their interests affected by the proposed development. If this seems possible, they should be consulted.
ACTION **C248**	Check with relevant authorities concerning highways, drainage, water, gas and electricity, etc. and note requirements for plant and meter housings, substations, etc.

C

ACTION **C249**	Agree with the client the need and/or arrangements for discussions with authorised users in developing the Project Brief and the Outline Proposals. Consult with authorised users.
NOTE	*Failure to agree party wall awards can lead to delays in start of work on site. Establish at an early stage whether notices under the Party Wall etc. Act 1996 will be needed.*
	Note that consultations with users or third parties, and party wall matters, do not form part of the Services under S-Con-07 unless identified under 'Other Services'.

C260 Approvals/consents

ACTION **C261**	Prepare an application for outline planning permission if appropriate and not yet obtained, and submit application if instructed by the client. Advise the client if this application relates to a listed building or building in a conservation area, and action accordingly.
ACTION **C262**	Submit applications for necessary approvals or consents required from third parties if instructed by the client.
NOTE	*Applications for outline planning permission and approval of landlords, funders, etc. do not form part of the Services under S-Con-07 unless identified under 'Other Services'.*

C290 Cost planning

ACTION **C291**	Provide information to QS for initial cost plan and cash flow projection (or prepare an approximation of construction cost if appointed to do so).	SEE ALSO **Fig. C1**
ACTION **C292**	Compare initial cost plan and cash flow forecast with the latest approved cost.	

ACTION **C293**	Discuss with the consultant team and the client the effect of major design decisions on the allocations within the cost plan before they are taken.
	NOTE *An increase in cost of one element, e.g. for a sophisticated external wall cladding system, may require complementary savings in other areas such as the mechanical services installation. Changes in the initial cost plan may require adjustment of budget and fees, and these changes should be agreed with the client.*
ACTION **C294**	Report to the client on cost matters at agreed intervals.

NOTE *If procurement is through design and build:*

- *for a contractor client: provide information to the contractor's estimators for costing out design proposals.*

C300	**General Procedures**

ACTION **C301**	Regularly check progress against the timetable for services.
ACTION **C302**	Continue resource control procedures for job: • Check expenditure against the office job cost allocation for Stage C. • Monitor fee income against projected fee income.
ACTION **C303**	Report regularly to the client on fees and expenses incurred, and submit accounts at agreed intervals.
ACTION **C304**	Check that the client settles all accounts promptly.
ACTION **C305**	Keep careful records of all conversations, consultations and design team meetings. File all notes and sketches prepared during the outline design process. Keep all manufacturers' or trade literature to which reference was made. It might be needed later as proof of the 'state of the art' at the time.

C400 Stage Outputs

Check that all the agreed outputs have been produced before the conclusion of Stage C, which might include the following:

SEE ALSO
Fig. C1

- partially developed Project Brief

- Outline Proposals – these should show the design sufficiently developed for the client to comprehend, comment on and approve the proposals. A diagrammatic analysis of requirements, use of site, solutions to functional and circulation problems, relationship of spaces, massing, construction and environmental methods may be included. Refer to the *RIBA Plan of Work: Multi-Disciplinary Services*

- an estimate of the construction cost sufficient to allow a cost plan to be prepared

- where agreed, special presentation material

NOTE   *If procurement is through design and build:*

- *for an employer client: outline proposals for Employer's Requirements*

- *for a contractor client: outline drawings for contractor's proposals*

Supplementary Material

C/SM1: Design and build documentation

Employer's Requirements

The amount of information to be included in the Employer's Requirements can vary enormously. A straightforward project requiring a relatively simple design solution which can be left largely to the contractor may need little more than basic details of site and accommodation. With a more complex problem, or a design which needs sensitivity of detail, the Employer's Requirements might extend to a full scheme design.

The number and detail of documents which make up the Employer's Requirements will be influenced by considerations such as:

- how much design control the employer wishes to retain, for example in the interests of maintenance programmes or because of functional requirements;
- whether the employer regards the process as more of a develop and construct operation, where only constructional details are left in the hands of the contractor;
- whether contractor's standard unit types will form the basis of the scheme;
- whether the employer will require design continuity via novation or a 'consultant switch';
- whether the employer has appointed a planning supervisor and whether a pre-tender Health and Safety Plan exists.
- Generally the Requirements will always need to include basic information, such as the following:
- site information and requirements (e.g. boundaries, topography, known subsoil conditions, existing services);
- site constraints (e.g. limitations of access, storage) and relevant easements or restrictive covenants;
- topographical surveys;
- geotechnical reports;
- planning permission obtained or conditions known (contractors will not usually tender until outline planning permission has been obtained);
- reports on other statutory consultations;
- existing Health and Safety Files, client's health and safety policy documents;
- functional nature of the building(s) (e.g. kind and number of units) and accommodation requirements;

- schematic layout of the building (or more developed design as appropriate);
- specific requirements as to forms of construction, materials, services, finishes, equipment, etc;
- specification information, probably including performance specifications;
- room data sheets;
- equipment and fitting schedules;
- details of special programming requirements (e.g. phased completion);
- contract data or special requirements (e.g. named sub-contractors, as built information);
- requirements concerning contractor's design liability, insurance cover, design team, requirement to use employer's designers, etc;
- clear statement of the extent of information and detail to be included in the Contractor's Proposals;
- content and form of the Contract Sum Analysis.

It is generally accepted that too specific an approach over design and constructional matters, or the specifying of proprietary systems and materials may reduce the contractor's design liability in the event of a failure.

Contractor's Proposals

These will be in direct response to the Employer's Requirements. Architects acting as consultants to a Contractor Client will first need to check the information provided to establish whether it is adequate. A query list is often necessary to obtain clarification on matters of conflict or omission.

Submissions sometimes take the form of an A3 brochure, and typically include the following:

- design drawings (e.g. site layout, floor plans, elevations, principal sections, some detailed drawings, landscaping);
- structural details (e.g. foundation and structure general arrangement drawings);
- mechanical services (e.g. layouts of ducts, pipe runs, schematic indications for all systems);
- electrical services (e.g. floor layouts showing lighting, power, alarms);
- specifications (e.g. particular for trades prescription and performance, general specification for workmanship, materials, finishes);
- programme (e.g. bar chart);
- method statements (e.g. general organisational matters and in particular Health and Safety Plan proposals).
- The tender figure will usually be required to be made separately. With it will be the Contract Sum Analysis.

- The structure of the Contract Sum Analysis will be in accordance with the Employer's Requirements. A typical breakdown could be:
- Design work
- Preliminaries
- Health and safety provisions
- Demolition
- Excavation
- Concrete
- Brickwork and blockwork
- Roofing and cladding
- Woodwork
- Structural steelwork
- Metalwork
- Mechanical and plumbing services
- Electrical services
- Glazing
- Painting and decorating
- Drainage and external works.

C/SM2: Consultant team roles

Quantity surveyor

The QS can assist the consultant team in reviewing financial aspects of the Outline Proposals and monitoring costs against the budget. He or she should be involved continuously and should report regularly at consultant team meetings.

The QS will evaluate the Strategic Brief and advise on the cost implications of design and energy options. He or she will prepare an initial cost plan and cash flow forecast, relying on input from other consultant team members.

Structural engineer

The engineer can work with the architect to develop structural concepts which are integral with the overall design in the Outline Proposals. He or she will visit the site and advise on the structural constraints it imposes, and advise on surveys needed, for example where there are special conditions such as contaminated land. The structural engineer can advise on environmental issues such as excavation and landfill. He or she should also liaise with services engineers to ensure integrated design. Priorities should be established and conflicts resolved at design team meetings.

Building services engineers

At Outline Proposals stage, the architect will take into account orientation, climatic and other environmental factors. There will also be a need to establish performance, installation costs and costs in use. The services consultants can play an important role in contributing to an integrated design approach, including consideration of sustainability issues, for example where there are special conditions such as contaminated land. The structural engineer can advise on environmental issues such as excavation and landfill. They will identify surveys required and initiate preliminary consultations with statutory authorities. They should contribute regularly to design team meetings.

Health and safety

All consultant team members should cooperate with the CDMC in carrying out risk assessments, and starting to prepare material for inclusion in the Health and Safety File and the pre-tender Health and Safety Plan.

Figures

Figure C1: Specimen cost plan / budget estimate

Job no: Job title:

Cost plan / budget estimate

		Cost of elements	Cost per m² gross floor area	Element shown as % of whole
Substructure				
Superstructure	Frame			
	Upper floors			
	Roof			
	Stairs			
	External cladding			
	Windows and external doors			
	Internal partitions			
	Internal doors and windows			
Internal finishes	Ceiling finishes			
	Wall finishes			
	Floor finishes			
Fittings	Furniture and fittings			
Services	Sanitary installation			
	Mechanical installation			
	Electrical installation			
	Special installations			
	Elevators and hoists			
	Builder's work			
	Builder's profit and attendance			
Building work	Sub-total			
Additional	Site works			
	Drainage			
	External services			
	Extra temporary works (phasing)			
	Inflation at 3%			
	Preliminaries at 5%			
Total	Excluding VAT and contingencies			

Design Development

STAGE DESCRIPTION

As defined in *RIBA Outline Plan of Work 2007*:

- Preparation of developed design to include structural and building services systems, updated outline specification and cost plan
- Completion of Project Brief
- *Application for detailed planning permission (may be moved to suit project requirements)*

CONTENTS

D

Stage Description

Generally at Stage D the Outline Proposals approved by the client are developed, and the Project Brief is completed. As lead consultant, the architect will need to be satisfied that there are no insurmountable problems ahead concerning the integration of the consultants' proposals into the overall design concept. As 'Designer', within the meaning of that term in the CDM Regulations, the architect will also have to be sure that all health and safety implications have been properly considered at this stage.

With design and build, where the architect is acting for an employer client, Stage D might cover design formulation to the extent necessary for inclusion as part of the Employer's Requirements. If the project has been tendered at an early stage in the development of the design, Stage D may involve the architect in assessing the contractor's design proposals and reporting to the employer client.

With a contractor client, the architect may be involved in the development of the design information already included as part of the contractor's proposals. The development of Detailed Proposals will probably not take place until there is confirmation that the contractor's bid has been approved, or a second stage tender is invited.

Where management procurement is followed, there will still need to be an overall design scheme even though it is anticipated that the detailed development will be phased. Thought should be given to how the works packages will be broken down, as this in turn might influence some design decisions.

Key Obligations

(from RIBA Agreements 2007: Standard Agreements (S-Con-07): Schedule of Design Services (SS-DS-07))

Contribute to completion of the Project Brief.

Investigate effect of statutory standards and construction safety on Concept Design.

Consult statutory authorities.

Develop the approved Concept Design to show spatial arrangements, type of construction, materials, appearance and detailed proposals for structural and building services systems and updated outline specifications.

Provide information for estimate of relevant cost.

Prepare and submit to client a Stage D report.

Prepare and submit an application for detailed planning permission.

D

D100   Preliminary Issues

D110   Information required

Check that all the information necessary during Stage D is available, which might include the following:

- partially developed Project Brief, derived from Strategic Brief

- Stage C Outline Proposals as accepted by the client in written confirmation, incorporating any agreed design changes

- further information as requested by the architect and supplied by the client

- notes, sketches and details made on visits to other projects

- relevant published material, technical information, etc.

- results of tests conducted during Stage C

- relevant legislation, circulars or guides

- further contributions, information and recommendations from consultants and specialists

- initial cost plan prepared by quantity surveyor

D120   Appointment

ACTION
D121

Establish scope, content and context for Stage D activities.

Put it into context, particularly if previous stages were undertaken by others. If possible, establish whether material produced now is likely to be acted upon by others taking over subsequent stages.

ACTION **D122**	If coming new to the project at this stage in the Plan of Work: • Ascertain that relevant Pre-Agreement and earlier Stage checks have been carried out. • Allow for familiarisation and reviewing of all usable material when agreeing fees and timetable with the client. • Confirm the role of the architect in relation to the rest of the consultant team. • Ensure that you have adequate professional indemnity insurance cover in accordance with ARB and RIBA requirements.
ACTION **D123**	Check that the client's instruction to proceed has been given and confirmed in writing.
ACTION **D124**	Check that the client has settled all accounts submitted to date.
ACTION **D125**	Check appointing documents with respect to services and fees. • If the extent of professional services for Stage D is not yet settled, agree with the client and confirm in writing. • If the methods and levels of charging for Stage D are not yet settled, agree with the client and confirm in writing.
ACTION **D126**	Assess office resources needed for Stage D and ensure that they are available and adequate.
ACTION **D127**	Carry out checks for compliance with in-house quality management procedures, including updated project quality plan.
ACTION **D128**	Review application of practice procedures to project.

D130	Client

ACTION D131	Check whether the client has confirmed in writing acceptance of the Outline Proposals submitted at Stage C. Establish points to be discussed and developed during Stage D.
ACTION D132	Advise the client on the need to appoint further consultants and specialists.
ACTION D133	Alert the client about any matters raised during discussions with statutory or other bodies which might affect the proposals. Explain the implications, and discuss what actions should be taken.
ACTION D134	Alert the client to the design implications arising out of health and safety legislation (e.g. circulation, design of workstations, environmental comfort, etc.) and implications for future maintenance, repair and replacement.
ACTION D135	Check that all information requested from the client concerning the site or existing buildings has been supplied.
ACTION D136	Ask the client for information and requirements concerning processes, plant and other installations, room layouts and equipment, etc. and record this information appropriately, if not already included in the Project Brief. Check on particular requirements concerning the life expectancy of components, fittings and installations, and performance requirements for environmental and services aspects, etc.
ACTION D137	Check whether the client wishes the project to be planned to allow for phasing of completion or completion to a particular sequence. This might have design implications.
ACTION D138	Check whether the client has decided the method of procurement, and confirm any decision in writing. If no decision is reached, explain the importance of reaching a decision before the detailed design is developed. This procurement method could affect the amount and type of design information needed at this stage.

D

D150	Consultant team

ACTION D151	Establish or review project quality management procedures in concert with relevant procedures of all consultant team members.	
ACTION D152	Check scope of professional services agreed with other consultants as they are appointed.	SEE ALSO **D/SM1**
ACTION D153	Agree input to the Stage by consultant team members.	
ACTION D154	Confirm Stage timetable for services, and note its relationship to the project timetable as agreed with the client. The timetable should show critical points by which information from the client and consultant team members will be required.	
ACTION D155	Confirm programme and pattern for consultant team meetings.	
ACTION D156	Appraise input from specialist firms, including potential subcontractors and suppliers.	
ACTION D157	Confirm arrangements for communication between client, CDM coordinator, project manager and design leader.	
ACTION D158	Monitor, coordinate and integrate input from consultant team members and specialists.	
NOTE	*Maintain close collaboration with consultants and specialists. The architect might not be responsible for their individual performances, but will be responsible for the coordination and integration of their work into the overall design.*	
ACTION D159	Check the designers' cooperation with the CDM coordinator with respect to the Health and Safety Plan and File.	
NOTE	*As lead consultant or design leader, the architect has an obligation to check that every designer pays regard to the CDM Regulations and avoids foreseeable risks, or takes steps to combat them at source when designing.*	

D200	Stage Activities

D210	Developing the Project Brief and the Design

ACTION D211	Review with the consultant team the client's response to Stage C Outline Proposals and decide what action is necessary.

ACTION D212	Review with the team the developing Project Brief. Check that the Stage C changes have been recorded, authorised by the client and dealt with by the change control procedures established (e.g. those set out in the project quality plan).

ACTION D213	Check that the brief, as presently developed, still meets the client's stated objectives. Further amendments should be agreed with the client and confirmed in writing.
NOTE	*The client must be advised that the Project Brief will be finalised during Stage D and warned that any modifications thereafter could mean abortive work and additional expense.*

ACTION D214	Obtain codes, standards, digests, etc. relevant to the project.
NOTE	*When designing to meet legislative standards or codes of practice, these must be the current versions.*

ACTION D215	Obtain project-specific information from potential subcontractors and suppliers.
NOTE	*When adopting proprietary systems or components for a design, take care that proposals will satisfy British Standards or other technical standards prescribed. Manufacturers' test results, as published, might relate to tests carried out under circumstances quite unlike those which might apply to a particular project. Check that products specified are suitable for the purpose and location, and obtain verification, certificates and warranties, as appropriate, before making a design commitment.*

ACTION D216	Coordinate and integrate information from QS, other consultants and specialists.

ACTION **D217**	Finalise Project Brief.	**SEE ALSO** **D/SM2**
NOTE	*During this Stage it is wise to draft preliminary specification notes, and to collate information as it comes to hand. Specification writing is part of the design process, and should be undertaken by the designer.*	

ACTION **D218**	Develop the Design. When developing the Design it will be necessary to make regular checks against the Brief as last updated. It is all too easy to overlook small but crucial requirements in the excitement of designing.

ACTION **D219**	Advise the client about any proposals to introduce innovative design or construction ideas or the specifying of relatively new materials, and ask the client to confirm awareness of these in writing.

ACTION **D220**	Undertake design review as appropriate.

ACTION **D221**	Finalise the Design. The presentation to the client of Stage D proposals is particularly important. Establish early how this is to be effected, and prepare the material accordingly. It will usually entail a written report and visual material. It may require an oral presentation.	**SEE ALSO** **D/SM3**
NOTE	*At the conclusion of Stage D, get the satisfied client to 'sign off' the Design and the Project Brief. Clearly, beyond this point any changes which are client-originated might mean abortive work and additional expense.*	

ACTION **D222**	Prepare report and submit to client.

D230   Inspections/tests

ACTION **D231**	Make further site/building visits as authorised.

| ACTION D232 | Arrange to inspect similar projects elsewhere if appropriate, perhaps accompanied by the client. Appraise and analyse the schemes. It would be wise to check first that expenditure is authorised by the client. |

| ACTION D233 | Arrange for testing, and record and analyse results if instructed by the client. These tests might include production prototypes, mock-ups, sample components and panels to be tested under specified conditions and to stipulated methods as appropriate, for example testing for structural performance, durability, consistency, etc. of components, fittings and finishes. |

NOTE *Surveys, inspections or specialist investigations and preparation of special models do not form part of the Services under Conditions of Appointment CA-S-07 unless identified under 'Other Services'.*

D240 Consultations

| ACTION D241 | Hold further meetings with statutory bodies as necessary. |

| ACTION D242 | Discuss with the planning officer any difficulties or conditions arising from an outline planning permission, and any problems likely to occur with a full planning application. Check whether the authority operates particular planning policies, issues its own supplementary guidance notes, etc. |

| ACTION D243 | Enquire whether the planning authority requires information additional to that of the usual form of application for full planning permission, and whether additional copies could speed up the consultation process. |

| ACTION D244 | Enquire whether it is possible to have representation at the planning committee at which the application is considered, should this be thought desirable. |

ACTION D245	Continue discussions with building control and the fire authorities over matters where overall design could be fundamentally affected, e.g. compartmentation, atrium design, fire resistance of elements, escape routes, smoke lobbies, active systems such as sprinklers, etc.
ACTION D246	Consult insurers, as appropriate, regarding the application of codes of practice or design guides relating to fire safety which might have design implications, e.g. compartmentation, atrium design, fire resistance of elements, active systems such as sprinklers, etc.
ACTION D247	Check health and safety legislation requirements likely to affect detailed planning. Continue to cooperate with the CDM coordinator and other designers over design implications of the pre-tender Health and Safety Plan required under the CDM Regulations.
ACTION D248	Continue checks with relevant authorities for highways, drainage, water, gas, electricity supplies, etc.
ACTION D249	Consult further with user clients, third parties and adjoining owners, if authorised. If instructed, issue party wall notices as soon as the proposals are sufficiently finalised, on behalf of client.
NOTE	*Consultations with users or third parties, and for party wall matters, do not form part of the Services under Conditions of Appointment CA-S-07 unless identified under 'Other Services'.*

D260   Approvals/consents

ACTION D261	Check whether necessary third-party consents are being obtained.

ACTION D262	Prepare and submit application for approval of reserved matters following an outline planning permission if appropriate.	

ACTION D263	Prepare and submit application for full planning permission, listed building consent and conservation area consent as relevant and if instructed by client. Ensure that all applications are accompanied by relevant documents including a cheque from the client for the appropriate fee.	SEE ALSO **A-B/SM4**

ACTION D264	Prepare and submit application for express consent to display an advertisement, application or notification to fell or lop trees covered by a tree preservation order or in a conservation area, as relevant.	

D270 Contract

ACTION D271	Confirm in writing with the client the procurement method and type of contract to be adopted.

ACTION D272	Discuss with the client and consultant team whether any preliminary tender action for specialist subcontractors and suppliers will be required.

ACTION D273	Discuss with the client and consultant team whether any action will be needed on advance orders.

ACTION D274	Identify works packages where applicable.

ACTION D275	Identify any performance-specified work or contractor's designed portion items.

ACTION D276	Discuss with the client any particular requirements for phased or sectional completion.

D

D290	**Cost planning**

ACTION D291	Discuss with the consultant team and the client the effect of major design decisions on the allocations within the cost plan before they are taken.
NOTE	*There must be regular two-way exchange of information if designers are to keep within cost targets or limits.*

ACTION D292	Provide the QS with information on the cost plan and cash flow projection (or prepare a cost estimate if appointed to do so).

ACTION D293	Report to the client on cost matters at agreed intervals.

NOTE	*If procurement is through design and build:*

- *for a contractor client: provide information to other consultants and contractors' estimators to cost detailed proposals.*

D300	**General Procedures**

ACTION D301	Check progress against the timetable for services regularly.

ACTION D302	Continue resource control procedures for job:

- Check expenditure against the office job cost allocation for Stage D.

- Monitor fee income against projected fee income.

ACTION D303	Report regularly to the client on fees and expenses incurred, and submit accounts at agreed intervals.

ACTION D304	Check that the client settles all accounts promptly.

D400   Stage Outputs

Check that all agreed outputs have been produced before the conclusion of Stage D, which might include the following:

SEE ALSO
D/SM1

- Project Brief developed from the Strategic Brief

- Detailed Proposals showing coordinated design intentions, site layout, planning and spatial arrangements, elevational treatment, construction and environmental systems and buildability

- developed proposals for existing, perhaps historic, buildings with information from conservators and other consultants

- a firm cost plan including a cash flow forecast

- prototypes, mock-ups, models, sample panels, etc.

- proposals developed sufficiently to allow an application for full planning permission/listed building consent/conservation area consent, etc. as applicable

---

NOTE   *If procurement is through design and build:*

- *for an employer client: Detailed Proposals for incorporation into Employer's Requirements (part of Stages D–G).*

- *for a contractor client: further notes, sketches, details and drawings as necessary to develop the scheme included in the contractor's proposals (part of Stages D–E).*

D

Supplementary Material

D/SM1: Consultant team roles

Cost consultant

The cost consultant should collaborate with the architect and other consultants to develop and refine the full cost plan as the design is developed and outline specification notes are prepared.

The cost consultant will prepare an elemental cost plan followed by a firm cost plan and cash flow forecast, relying on input from other consultant team members, and will advise on cost effects of compliance with statutory requirements. The QS should contribute information and advice for inclusion in the Stage D report to the client.

Structural engineer

The structural engineer should collaborate in developing the design, and advise on structural options and preferred solutions. The architect is responsible for coordination and integration into the overall design concept. This will include checking that structural proposals are compatible with the space and access requirements of the services installations.

The structural engineer should produce the initial structural design, prescribe profiles, basic specifications and building tolerances, define basic rules for voids and holes which might need to be provided and which might affect the structure, and take steps as necessary to establish compliance with statutory requirements. They will provide information for the elemental and firm cost plan, and should contribute information and advice for inclusion in the Stage D report to the client.

D

D/SM2: Project Brief: final checklist

By the end of Stage D the brief should be finalised and signed off by the client. The Project Brief should normally address the following:

(a) the aim of the design, including:

- prioritised project objectives
- accommodation requirements, including disabled access policy
- space standards
- environmental policy, including energy
- environmental performance requirements
- image and quality
- flexibility to accommodate future reorganisation
- allowance for future expansion or extension
- lifespan for structure, elements, installations
- operational and maintenance requirements
- special considerations (e.g. security)

(b) the site, including details of accessibility and planning

- site constraints (physical and legal)
- legislative constraints

(c) the functions and activities of the client

- schedule of functions or processes
- activities
- spatial relationships
- schedule of installations

(d) the structure of the client organisation

(e) the size and configuration of the facilities

(f) options for environmental delivery and control

(g) servicing options and specification implications, e.g. security, deliveries, access, workplace, etc.

(h) outline specifications of general and specific areas

(i) a budget for all elements

(j) the procurement process

(k) the project execution plan

(l) key targets for quality, time and cost, including milestones for decisions

(m) method for assessing and managing risks and validating design proposals

D/SM3: Design development presentation

Presentation to the client at Stage D will be in the most appropriate form, or may have to be in a form directed by the client. A decision should be made as early as possible, and might be influenced by context.

The medium of presentation

Decide how presentation of the scheme design is to be made, for example by:

- the architect in person
- written report and drawings
- electronic means

The intended recipients

Establish who is to be the immediate recipient of the scheme design presentation (e.g. client in person or client body committee) and whether the same material will also have a secondary presentation (e.g. to the planning committee, public meetings, user client groups).

The end users

Establish the use to which presentation material is likely to be put initially and in the longer term (e.g. for public display, fund raising, media coverage). This might require production of specially commissioned material, or simply multiple copies of the original material.

The content

The content of information to be presented and the media to be used might include, for example:

Written report

- presenting facts for information
- suggesting and comparing solutions
- making recommendations
- including, or accompanied by, illustrations, drawings and a financial report

Drawings

- orthographic plans at all levels
- elevations and cross-sections
- perspectives, etc. to give a realistic view of the building exterior
- computer-generated visual images or analytical diagrams

Models

- block model (working tool)
- presentation model to show architectural quality, form and colour, landscape setting, etc.
- detail model of building part or particular feature, etc.
- interior arrangement model to show spaces, arrangements, furniture layouts, etc.
- computer-generated models

Multimedia

- Computer animation, video, CD

The scheme design presentation will also be influenced by factors such as:

- whether material is to be produced in-house or by outside professionals
- whether the presentation is covered by a budget allocation, or is to be paid for direct by the client
- the anticipated life of the material and its subsequent storage
- costs associated with circulation, transport (particularly if overseas), insurance, etc.

D

Technical Design

STAGE DESCRIPTION

As defined in *RIBA Outline Plan of Work 2007*:

■ Preparation of technical design(s) and specifications, sufficient to coordinate components and elements of the project and information for statutory standards and construction safety

E

CONTENTS

CONTINUES

134

CONTENTS (CONTINUED)

Stage Description

Generally at Stage E the approved design is developed in technical detail, the last stage in the design development before the production information is prepared. The technical design will include the required construction details, choice of materials and standards of workmanship. Consultation with the client will be needed throughout the process. The client may be expected to contribute information or comments on finishes, furnishings and equipment. Design work by consultants and specialists must be coordinated, and relevant information passed to the planning supervisor for inclusion in the Health and Safety Plan and File. Cost checks are essential at this stage to ensure that the design development does not exceed budgetary limits or depart from the approved cost estimate.

In design and build procurement with an employer client, the design will be developed to the level of detail previously agreed. It is relatively rare for the employer client to require technical design as part of the Employer's Requirements. However, some exploratory detail design is often necessary before the Employer's Requirements can be finished.

With a contractor client, technical design will usually closely overlap production information. It may overlap for inclusion in the contractor's proposals, or if the contract has already been let, the information may be solely for the contractor's design development. The detail design development will be associated with the work of other consultants to the contractor, specialist subcontractors and the estimators within the contractor organisation.

With the management procurement approach, the technical design is more difficult to resolve. A significant proportion will depend on the input of the specialists involved with the works packages, and not all their contributions will be available at this stage. Stage E for management contracting cannot be equated with traditional procurement, as much will remain to be resolved after the contract and works packages have been let. Great reliance has to be placed on the management contractor or construction manager, and an early appointment will help the technical design development. Close attention should be given to the appropriate number of packages and control maintained to minimise the risk of overlap or duplication. Monitoring of detail design will continue well into the construction phase, and the Health and Safety File might require regular adjustment.

E

Key Obligations

(from RIBA Agreements 2007: Standard Agreements (S-Con-07): Schedule of Design Services (SS-DS-07))

Consult statutory authorities on developing design.

Prepare technical designs, calculations and specifications sufficient to coordinate components and elements of the project including information for statutory standards and construction safety.

Provide information for updating estimate of relevant cost.

Prepare and submit to client a Stage E report.

| **E100** | **Preliminary Issues** |

| **E110** | **Information required** |

Check that all information necessary during Stage E is available:

- Project Brief as accepted by the client in written confirmation, incorporating any agreed amendments

- Detailed Proposals as accepted by the client in written confirmation, incorporating any agreed amendments

- cost plan prepared by quantity surveyor

- published material and technical information including samples relevant to the project

- results of tests conducted during Stage D

- relevant legislation

- further contributions, information and recommendations from consultants and specialists including possible subcontractors and suppliers

| **E120** | **Appointment** |

ACTION
E121

Establish scope, content and context for Stage E activities. Put it into context, particularly previous stages undertaken by others. If possible establish whether material produced now is likely to be acted upon by others taking over subsequent Stages.

ACTION **E122**	If coming new to the project at this Stage in the Plan of Work: • Ascertain that relevant Pre-Agreement and earlier Stage checks have been carried out. • Allow for familiarisation and reviewing of all usable Stage A–D material when agreeing fees and timetable with the client. • Confirm the role of the architect in relation to the rest of the consultant team. • Ensure that you have adequate professional indemnity insurance cover in accordance with ARB and RIBA requirements.
ACTION **E123**	Check that the client's instruction to proceed has been given and confirmed in writing.
ACTION **E124**	Check that the client has settled all accounts submitted to date.
ACTION **E125**	Check appointing documents with respect to services and fees. • If the services, cost or time targets are different from the agreement with the client, agree a formal variation by letter or deed as appropriate. • If the extent of professional services for Stage E is not settled, agree with the client and confirm in writing. • If the methods and levels of charging for Stage E are not yet settled, agree with the client and confirm in writing.
ACTION **E126**	Assess office resources needed for Stage E and ensure that they are available and adequate.
ACTION **E127**	Carry out checks for compliance with in-house quality management procedures, including updated project quality plan. Review application of practice procedures to project.

E130	**Client**

ACTION E131	Check whether the client has confirmed in writing acceptance of the Project Brief and Detailed Proposals submitted at Stage D. Establish points to be discussed and developed during Stage E.
ACTION E132	It is important to remind the client that any changes to the approved Project Brief which are client-originated might mean abortive work, additional expense and delays.
ACTION E133	Continue discussion with the client on more detailed aspects of procurement, and confirm decisions in writing. The decisions will affect the finalisation of the design during this Stage, the amount and type of design information needed at this Stage and the role of the consultants.
NOTE	*The client should be given reasonable notice to supply detailed final requirements concerning access, facilities, furnishings, fittings, etc. Likewise, take into account users' requirements as relevant.*
ACTION E134	Check whether client has given authority for any preliminary tender action for specialist subcontractors and suppliers that will be required, and confirm in writing.
ACTION E135	Advise the client on the need to appoint further consultants and specialists.
ACTION E136	Ensure that the client is alerted to the possible need to appoint party wall surveyors.

E150	**Consultant team**

ACTION E151	Establish or review project quality management procedures in concert with relevant procedures of all consultant team members.
ACTION E152	Check scope of professional services agreed with other consultants as they are appointed.

ACTION **E153**	Agree input to the Stage by consultant team members.

NOTE	*Remember that the procurement method chosen will greatly affect the amount of detail design information necessary at this stage.*

ACTION **E154**	Confirm Stage timetable for services, and note its relationship to the project timetable as agreed with the client.

ACTION **E155**	Confirm arrangements for communication between client, CDM coordinator, project manager and design leader.

ACTION **E156**	Confirm arrangements for communication between consultant team members.

ACTION **E157**	Have an agreed policy for issuing and exchanging drawings and other information.

ACTION **E158**	Establish information flow schedule and delivery programme.

ACTION **E159**	Have an agreed policy for coordinating information on drawings and between documents. Coordinated Project Information should be introduced at the earliest possible stage in information preparation.	SEE ALSO **E/SM1** **FIGS. E1-E6**
NOTE	*Be careful when using networked CAD systems that there is a clear procedure for updating and circulating base drawings to be used by the whole team.*	
	There must be an organised flow of information between the architect and other consultants, particularly with the QS.	

ACTION **E160**	Confirm programme and pattern for consultant team meetings.

ACTION **E161**	Confirm with consultant team members arrangements for inviting specialist tenders.

ACTION **E162**	Monitor, coordinate and integrate input from consultant team members. The architect needs to bring both design and management skills to Stage E. Collaboration with other consultant team members and coordination of their contributions is often difficult to achieve in practice.
ACTION **E163**	Check the designers' cooperation with the planning supervisor with respect to the Health and Safety Plan and File.
ACTION **E163**	Check that any design changes now instructed are recorded and subject to established control procedures.
NOTE	*No consultant team members should attempt to make decisions unilaterally!*

E

E200	**Stage Activities**

E210	**Developing the Project Brief and Technical Design**

ACTION **E211**	Review with the consultant team the client's response to Stage D Design and decide what action is necessary. See also checklist in S-Con-07.
ACTION **E212**	Appraise input from specialist firms, including potential subcontractors and suppliers.
ACTION **E213**	Coordinate and integrate information from consultant team members.
ACTION **E214**	Obtain the client's approval of materials and finishes. Obtain samples, etc. and submit to the client for comment. Prepare special presentation panels, etc. for the client.

| ACTION E215 | Draft preliminary notes for bills/spec/schedules of work. |
| | This should be done systematically as further materials are chosen and standards of workmanship set. |

| ACTION E216 | Undertake design review as appropriate. |
| | Complete technical design. |

| ACTION E217 | Prepare report and submit to client. |

NOTE | *If procurement is through design and build:*

- *for an employer client: check whether the client has confirmed in writing acceptance of proposals and information supplied so far to form part of the Employer's Requirements.*

- *for a contractor client: check whether the client has confirmed in writing acceptance of design proposals to form part of the contractor's proposals.*

E230   Inspections/tests

| ACTION E231 | Make such visits as necessary to supply sources (e.g. quarries, brickyards, stoneyards) and manufacturing sources (e.g. foundries, factories, workshops) before making final design choices. |

| ACTION E232 | Arrange for further tests to be conducted on components, panels and finishes, if appropriate and authorised by the client. |

E240   Consultations

| ACTION E241 | Review with the design team implications of any conditions attached to full planning permission. |

ACTION E242	Discuss with the planning officer the implications arising from any planning permission conditions. If permission was refused, discuss the reasons for the refusal and prepare, for the client, recommendations as to the best course of action.
NOTE	*Revision of documents to comply with planning or other statutory authority requirements does not form part of the Services under Conditions of Appointment CA-S-07 unless identified under 'Other Services'.*

ACTION E243	Continue discussions with the building control and fire authorities before making a formal application for approval under the Building Regulations.

ACTION E244	Review adequacy of information on building services from statutory undertakers for detail design.

ACTION E245	Continue discussions with relevant authorities for highways, drainage, water, gas, electricity supplies, etc. on matters concerning detail design. Check adequacy of information on building services from statutory undertakers for detail design.

ACTION E246	Consult insurers as appropriate regarding the application of codes of practice or design guides relating to construction, materials, standards and finishes in detail design, and their requirements for fire prevention during site operations which might have design implications.

ACTION E247	Consult user clients/third parties, if authorised.

ACTION E248	If instructed, issue party wall notices on behalf of the client.
NOTE	*Consultations with users or third parties, and party wall matters, do not form part of the Services under Conditions of Appointment CA-S-07 unless identified under 'Other Services'.*

E260	Approvals/consents

ACTION **E261**	In the event of a refusal of planning permission, amend the scheme and re-submit the application as appropriate.
NOTE	*Exceptional negotiations with planning or other statutory authorities do not form part of the Services under Conditions of Appointment CA-S-07 unless identified under 'Other Services'.*

ACTION **E262**	Check whether minor amendments to the Detailed Proposals at this Stage go beyond the scope of the planning permission granted. If so, it may be necessary to deposit amended drawings.

ACTION **E263**	Prepare a Building Notice for submission under the Building Regulations, or prepare an application for approval by deposit of Full Plans. Prepare a submission to an Approved Inspector for issue of an Initial Notice for acceptance by the local authority, if this is the chosen option.	SEE ALSO **F/SM4**
NOTE	*Application for Building Regulations approval is not included in the Conditions of Appointment CA-S-07 until Stage F, although 'statutory approvals' appears in Stage E and Stage F of the Plan of Work. In practice, it is advisable to submit for all necessary approvals at the earliest possible date. However, the Stage at which the submissions can be made will depend on how much detail the authority requires – there is an increasing tendency to ask for a high level of detail so that submission may not be possible until Stage F.*	

ACTION **E264**	Prepare material for submission to the client's insurers if necessary and if instructed by the client.

E270	Contract

NOTE	*The Conditions of Appointment CA-S-07 refer to tender action at Stage H only. In projects where there are to be many specialist subcontractors, particularly where these are undertaking some design obligations, it may be necessary to initiate some tender action of subcontractors at an earlier stage. This will enable design proposals to be integrated into the overall design and quotations to be checked against the cost plan. This information may be needed before the main contract tender documentation can be finalised at Stage G. Refer also to diagrams showing the relationship of stages in the* RIBA Outline Plan of Work 2007

ACTION E271	Review/update standing lists or register of specialist tenderers and check written confirmation from client. Check willingness and availability of firms included as listed subcontractors, and if necessary decide on additional names.	

ACTION E272	Initiate tender action for quotations from specialist subcontractors and suppliers if appropriate.	SEE ALSO **H/SM2**
	Check tender invitation documents for sending to specialists.	
	Invite further tenders as appropriate.	
	When inviting tenders for specialist subcontract work which includes a design element, make certain that the client consents in writing, and that their interests are properly protected by warranty.	

E

ACTION **E273**	Inspect tenders and information submitted by specialist subcontractors and suppliers. Refer specialist tenders to the planning supervisor and relevant consultants for comment. Refer all tenders to the QS for cost checking. Approve specialist tenders and notify all tenderers of this decision. NOTE *Follow meticulously the procedures stated in the main contract to be used for the appointment of specialist subcontractors.* *Only place advance orders with specialist subcontractors or suppliers as provided for in the subcontract documentation, and only if authorised in writing by the client, as advised by the planning supervisor.* Discuss list of potential main contractors (or construction managers if appropriate) with client and consultant team. Check whether the client holds a General List of Approved Contractors from which tenderers must be selected. Make preliminary enquiries with contractors if appropriate. NOTE *Tender lists should only include firms well known to the architect, or firms which have been satisfactorily investigated.*
ACTION **E274**	Discuss with the client tender procedures, including: • whether firms who wish to be considered as tenderers should complete a tendering questionnaire • whether the client will require tenderers to complete a non-collusion or other similar certificate SEE ALSO **H/SM1**
ACTION **E275**	Discuss with the client and the planning supervisor the tendering period and procedures to be followed in opening tenders, and notify the results.
ACTION **E276**	Continue discussion with the client on the inclusion of any special clauses or amendments to the contract. Remind the client of the need to take legal advice before amending standard forms of contract. Discuss with the client the implications of any advice obtained.

E290	Cost planning

ACTION E291	Discuss with the consultant team and the client the effect of detailed design decisions on the allocations within the cost plan before implementation.
ACTION E292	Provide information to QS for revision of the cost estimate and cash flow projection (or revise the cost estimate if appointed to do so).
ACTION E293	Report to the client on cost matters at agreed intervals.

NOTE *If procurement is through design and build:*

For a contractor client:

- *Provide any further necessary information to the contractor's estimators.*

- *Review estimates received from specialist firms, either direct or through consultants, for inclusion in tender documents or as basis for provisional sums.*

E300	**General Procedures**

ACTION E301	Check progress against the timetable for services regularly.
ACTION E302	Continue resource control procedures for job: - Check expenditure against the office job cost allocation for Stage E. - Monitor fee income against projected fee income.

E

ACTION E303	Report regularly to the client on fees and expenses incurred, and submit accounts at agreed intervals.

ACTION E304	Check that the client settles all accounts promptly.

E400   Stage Outputs

Check that all the agreed outputs have been produced before the conclusion of Stage E, which might include the following:

- detail design drawings

- specification notes (prescriptive and performance) on materials and workmanship, etc. and notes for draft preambles or preliminaries for bills of quantities/specification/ schedules of work

- further detailed information on proposals for existing, perhaps historic, buildings

- information for preparation of Full Plans submission for approval under the Building Regulations

- non-production information for use in dealings with third parties, landlords, tenants, funders, etc. (e.g. in connection with leases, boundaries, party walls, etc.)

 If procurement is through design and build:

- *for an employer client: detail design information for incorporation into Employer's Requirements (part of Stages D–G).*

- *for a contractor client: further design development drawings and design team members' work on scheme submitted in the contractor's proposals (part of Stages D–E).*

Supplementary Material

E/SM1: Design information – implications of procurement method

The production of information, its amount, type and timing, are likely to be directly affected by the procurement method chosen, and ultimately by the type of contract selected.

For example, the extent to which there is to be contractual reliance on drawings might determine their form and detail. Whether bills of quantities or schedules of work will be needed will depend on the form of contract and the nature of the work.

It is important to identify at detail design stage who will have responsibility for producing what information – architect, consultants, contractor, specialist firms, etc.

The more complex the pattern of information required, the greater the risk of omissions, errors and inconsistencies between documents. Greater, too, is the need for collaboration in order to bring about integration and coordination of design information.

Ideally all information necessary for the construction of the project should be completed before construction work begins. In practice this ideal is rarely, if ever, achieved, but if a great deal is left to be prepared during the construction stage, then very high levels of management skill will be needed from all those involved.

Even in traditional procurement it is rarely possible to bring a lump sum project to a fully designed state pre-tender. Most building contracts accept the need for further information to be issued during progress of the works.

With design and build, or management contracts, it is recognised that a substantial amount of detail design work will take place after the main contract has been let.

In an attempt to control the amount and flow of information, and recognising that everything will not always be available at the start of a contract, a schedule of information still to be provided is sometimes agreed beforehand by the architect and the contractor. This has now been embodied in many JCT standard form contracts as an optional 'Information Release Schedule'.

Sometimes the successful tenderer is required to inspect the documentation and provide the client with verification that it will be sufficient to carry out and complete the project. Then, should it be necessary to produce further drawings or calculations, this will be the contractor's risk. However, the architect will then

E

be involved in checking the contractor's submissions to ensure that detail design is not compromised.

Design information flow: traditional procurement

1. Origination

Design information can originate from:

- the architect
- design team members
- specialist subcontractors and suppliers
- the main contractor (to the extent provided for in the contract)

2. Coordination and integration

Responsibility for coordinating and integrating such information into the overall design rests with the architect as lead consultant, or design team leader.

3. Detail design work

Some detail design work is necessary for all projects and should be started as soon as practicable. The transition from the technical proposals of Stage E to the Stage F production information is not easily defined. There will inevitably be a measure of overlap which might vary from project to project. With small projects the two stages might be merged.

4. Design development

With traditional procurement, where a project is to be fully designed before work on site commences, Stage E provides an opportunity to develop and refine the design intentions. The scheme can be systematically explored and parts expanded to a larger scale in plan, section or three dimensions. Potentially awkward junctions can be identified and resolved. Zones may be introduced and a grid discipline imposed.

5. Avoidance of conflict and overlap

Design information originating from various sources should be coordinated, to eliminate any conflicts or duplication. It is normally the task of the lead consultant to check design coordination. A key example is the coordination required between structure and services, to make sure that different services are not competing for the same duct spaces, or that holes are not expected at critical structural points. Design integrity and quality should not need to be sacrificed because of the requirements of other design team members, but achieving acceptable compromise and satisfactory integration can be a demanding process.

Smaller projects which might need only a dozen or so drawings, and very limited input from consultants, are unlikely to present real problems in terms of integration and coordination.

Larger and more complex projects will need a more formalised set of procedures. The design concept is likely to be founded on a totally integrated approach. There should be an agreed strategy for the coordination of information between the architect and other consultant team members.

See *RIBA Outline Plan of Work* 'Fully designed project'.

Design information flow: design and build procurement

1. Origination

Design information can originate from:

- the employer client (through Employer's Requirements with input from their consultant team)
- the contractor client (through contractor's proposals and subsequent development of these, with input from their consultant team)

2. Coordination and integration

If acting as lead consultant or design leader appointed by either the employer client or the contractor client, responsibility for coordinating and integrating the relevant design information may rest with the architect, always depending on the terms of appointment.

3. Employer client's design in Employer's Requirements

Where an employer client includes a scheme devised by their own consultant team as part of the Employer's Requirements, some Stage E detail work might be relevant. The extent of the commitment should be agreed with the client before work is undertaken. In the event that novation or a 'consultant switch' is envisaged, particular care might be needed to establish design viability. The point of changeover for design liability from one client to the other must be carefully defined.

4. Contractor client's design in contractor's proposals

Where a contractor client is expected to offer a scheme design as part of the contractor's proposals, this may involve only a fairly limited design exercise, or require a more developed design approach, particularly in the case of two-stage tendering. Either way, some exploratory detail design work is necessary to establish the viability of the proposal. The extent of the commitment should be agreed with the client before work is started.

contractor's proposals sometimes entail the preparation of a considerable number of architectural drawings – general arrangement, plans, sections and elevations, sectional and elevational details and landscape proposals. There may also be full structural details and a substantial number of services drawings. Obviously effective coordination and integration of the information is very important.

5. Detail design work

Stage E, insofar as it might be relevant for a contractor client, could continue intermittently throughout the early stages of construction. It might be difficult to distinguish at times from production information work. Detail design might be subject to fairly liberal interpretation, with last-minute amendments, revisions or substitutions by the contractor client. The client might also have a particular preference for detail design solutions which are familiar, will wish to use materials or components which are available to suit the programme, and will wish to keep in line with the estimator's calculations.

Stage E, insofar as it might be relevant for an employer client, will probably apply mainly to the development of the Employer's Requirements. Once the contract has been let, any changes in these are likely to be costly and weighted heavily in the contractor's favour.

6. Avoidance of conflict

Once the contract is under way, should any conflict between the Employer's Requirements and the contractor's proposals emerge, then depending on the wording of the contract, the latter is likely to take precedence. Careful scrutiny at Stage E is therefore advisable, whether the architect is acting for the employer client or the contractor client.

See *RIBA Outline Plan of Work* 'Design and build project'.

Design information flow: management procurement

Management procurement is likely to be particularly suitable where the project is fairly large or complex, where there is need for early completion, and where the requirements of the client might change or perhaps only be formalised in detail during work on site. Design is still in the hands of the professional team. The management contractor is appointed early enough to advise the team on buildability but carries no responsibility for the design. As lead consultant or design leader, responsibility for coordinating and integrating information into the overall design rests with the architect, although considerable design input will normally come from the specialist works contractors.

1. Origination

Design information can originate from:

- the architect
- professional team members
- specialist works contractors

2. Detail design work

Two general lines of the design will be shown in the project drawings and project specification produced by the professional team. Some Stage E detail design is an essential precursor to information issued when inviting tenders for works packages.

Further detail design work will arise when the works contractors are appointed. Each discrete work package must be placed in the context of the overall design. The information flow can produce management problems if not effectively controlled. Risk of frustrated design work and perhaps abortive fabrication can occur unless agreed procedures are adopted by the management contractor and the professional team.

3. Coordination and integration

The management contractor can expect to be closely involved in the appointment of works contractors. This might be on the basis of developed detail drawings, specifications and perhaps bills of quantities. Drawings prepared by the works contractors will be mainly installation or shop drawings, and should be passed to the architect by the management contractor for inspection with regard to their integration and incorporation into the overall design.

See *RIBA Outline Plan of Work* 'Management Contract / Construction Management'.

E

Figure E1: Specimen checklist of necessary drawn information

Job no: Job title:

Drawn information checklist

Summary		Site layouts	
		General arrangements	
		drawings	

| **Substructure** | | Excavation | Foundations |
| | | Floors beds | Pile foundations |

Structure	**Primary**	External walls	Stairs and ramps
		Internal walls	Roofs
		Floors and galleries	Frames
	Secondary	External wall openings	Balustrades
		Internal wall openings	Suspended ceilings
		Floor openings	Roof openings
	Finishes	External wall finishes	Stair finishes
		Internal wall finishes	Ceiling finishes
		Floor finishes	Roof finishes

Services	**Piped and ducted**	Refuse disposal	Refrigeration
		Drainage	Space heating
		Hot and cold water	Ventilation and air conditioning
		Gases	
	Electrical	Power	Transport
		Lighting	Security
		Communications	

Fittings	**Fixtures**	Circulation	Sanitary
		General room	Cleaning
		Culinary	Storage
	Loose equipment	Circulation	Sanitary
		General room	Cleaning
		Culinary	Storage

External		Substructure	Services
		Structure	Fittings
		Finishes	

Register of Drawings

Most practices will already have a standard Register of Drawings (see Fig. E2a), which might record, among other things:

- job number and title
- drawing number, title, date, revisions (A, B, etc.)
- scale of drawing, size of drawing (A3, A4, etc.)
- number of copies sent, distribution, and date sent

Where recipients are to be charged for copies, the Register might also allow entries indicating the charge made and by whom payable. Great care must be taken to keep the register updated, particularly where networked CAD systems are being used.

E

Figure E2a: Specimen register of drawings

| Job no: | Job title: | | | |

Register of drawings

Drawing no.	Drawing title	Scale	Date	Notes

| Compiled by: | Date: | Sheet: |

Figure E2b: Specimen register of prints

Job no: Job title:

Register of prints

Drawing no.	Drawing title	Issued to	No. copies	Date	Change

Compiled by: Date: Sheet:

E

Schedules of drawings

Drawing schedules can be a convenient record for several purposes:

- for listing at the start of Stage E what drawings or drawn schedules need to be prepared
- for listing at the start of Stage F–G what production information needs to be prepared (see Fig. E4)
- for listing drawings or drawn schedules issued for tender purposes
- for listing necessary information still to be prepared by the architect and/or the contractor during progress of the works
- for listing drawings or drawn schedules supplied to the client on completion – either for record purposes or for incorporation in the Health and Safety File

Figure E3: Specimen schedule of drawings required

Job no: Job title:

Schedule of drawings required (prepared before drafting starts)

Drawing no.	Drawing title	Sheet size	Scale	Notes
L00	Site location plan	A3	1:1250	
01	Site plan	A1	1:200	
02	Site plan: contractor's fencing	A1	1:200	

Distribution: Date:

E

Drawings issued

Drawings should never normally be issued simply under cover of a compliments slip. It is better practice to use a drawing issue sheet (see Fig. E4) which indicates the purpose of the action and allows a proper record to be kept.

Drawings received

A practice should also have its standard record of drawings received. All incoming drawn or scheduled information should be entered, and the sheets might record among other things:

- job number and title
- drawing number, title, date, revision
- name of originator
- date received
- whether response required and if so by when
- response made and date achieved

Figure E4: Specimen architect's drawing issue sheet

Job no: Job title:

Architect's drawing issue sheet

Please find enclosed the drawings listed below.
Any errors or omissions should be notified immediatlely.

Distribution   No. copies

Purpose of issue   For information ☐   For comment ☐
                      For approval ☐   For cost check ☐

Drawing no.	Revision	Drawing title

Signed: Date:

E

Figure E5: Specimen record of drawings received

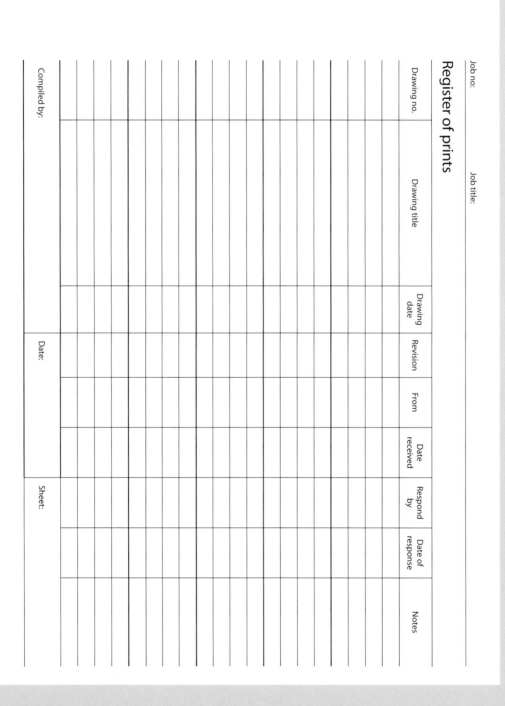

Design change notice

Drawings or other documents indicating proposed design changes should be circulated under cover of a change notice (see Fig. E6) which invites comments from recipients. These photocopied (if not sent in duplicate) forms should then be filed, and the action taken recorded. Following the adoption of design changes, amendments might be needed to the entries in the Register of Drawings.

E

Figure E6: Specimen design change notice and record

Job no: Job title:

Design change notice and record

To:

Enclosures: Please find enclosed the documents listed below.
                       Please enter comments, photocopy, and return original notice by

                       _____   (Date)

                       Issued by   Date:

Comments:

                       Signed   Date:

Implementation record   Change adopted YES/NO   Included in contract YES/NO

                       Covered by Architect's instruction   No.   issued   (date)

Production Information

STAGE DESCRIPTION

As defined in *RIBA Outline Plan of Work 2007*:

F1 Preparation of detailed information for construction
Application for statutory approvals*
F2 Preparation of further information for construction required under the
building contract
Review of information provided by contractors or specialists*

* These activities may be moved to suit project requirements

CONTENTS

Stage Description

Generally at Stage F the final proposals are translated into precise technical instructions sufficient to allow for pricing and for construction of the proposed works. This information will normally be conveyed by means of written descriptions, drawings and schedules. The *RIBA Outline Plan of Work* recognises that with many procurement routes some of this information may be prepared and provided after the main contract has been entered into, and the Stage is split into F1 and F2 accordingly.

Design and build procurement

Responsibility for production information in design and build procurement will depend on the particular circumstances. It would be very unusual for an employer client to arrange for production information direct, although they might retain a consultant team to monitor production information prepared and submitted by the contractor. Alternatively, the employer might require the continued use of their team by the successful contractor through a consultant switch or 'novation'. The contractor client will require production information to be prepared. An architect engaged in this context might well find it advisable to establish exactly how much work, how many drawings, etc. will be required before agreeing a programme or fee. The contractor might wish to impose conditions in respect of the method of structuring and supply of production information, preferred technical solutions, materials, etc.

Management procurement

With management procurement, the amount of production information available at the commencement of the project will be limited to the extent that much detail information will be supplied by the works contractors by way of shop or installation drawings. Nevertheless, the general production information will originate from the consultant team, and the process of coordinating and integrating information will continue throughout the construction of the project.

F

Key Obligations

(from RIBA Agreements 2007: Standard Agreements (S-Con-07): Schedule of Design Services (SS-DS-07))

F1

Prepare detailed information including specifications required for construction and/or tender purposes.

Prepare and make submissions (give Building Notice – except in Scotland).

Provide information for updating estimate of relevant cost.

Prepare and submit to client a Stage F1 report.

F2

Prepare further information for construction purposes.

Review design information provided by specialists or contractors.

F100	Preliminary Issues

F110	Information required

Check that all information necessary during Stage F is available:

- final proposals prepared during Stage E and any other stage information prepared by the other consultants, specialists, suppliers and the contractor and subcontractors

- any amendments recommended by local building control and fire authorities during consultations, particularly relating to construction details and fire prevention including finishes, that have not been incorporated into the Stage E information

NOTE

Under the Regulatory Reform (Fire Safety) Order 2005, the law does not require fire certificates but makes it the duty of

- *the person responsible for (non-domestic) premises*

- *employers or*

- *building constructors with a degree of control over premises*

to have a suitable and sufficient fire risk assessment in place

- technical information from manufacturers and recommendations or test results relevant to the particular use intended, context and location

- relevant legislation

F

F120	Appointment

ACTION **F121**	Establish scope and content for Stage F activities.

NOTE

Put this into context, particularly if previous stages were undertaken by others. If possible, establish whether material produced now is likely to be acted upon by others taking over subsequent stages.

If the appointment includes Stage L2 the architect must advise on requirements relating to occupation strategies and facilities management to be included in production information and provide information for revision of cost estimate.

If the appointment includes Stage L3 the architect must identify any changes to targets and their causes, identify services to be provided to the review by constructors and contribute to the Work Stage report.

ACTION **F122**	If coming new to the project at this stage in the Plan of Work:

- Ascertain that the relevant Pre-Agreement and earlier stage checks have been carried out.

- Agree fees and timetable with the client.

NOTE

Allow for familiarisation and reviewing of all usable material.

- Confirm the role of the architect in relation to the rest of the consultant team.

- Ensure that you have the necessary competency and resource to undertake the design work and to address the H&S issues likely to be involved in it.

- Request a copy of the project-specific, pre-construction health and safety information and review it.

- Advise the client of responsibilities under the CDM Regulations and ensure that a CDMC has been appointed.

NOTE

Where a project is notifiable, the regulations require that the client appoints a CDMC as soon as is practicable after initial design work or other preparation for construction work has begun. This would generally be at Stage C.

- Ensure that you have adequate professional indemnity insurance cover.

ACTION F123	Check that the client's instruction to proceed has been given and confirmed in writing.
ACTION F124	Check that the client has settled all accounts submitted to date.
ACTION F125	Check the appointing documents with respect to services and fees: • If the extent of professional services for Stage F is not yet settled, agree with the client and confirm in writing. • If the methods and levels of charging for Stage F are not yet settled, agree with the client and confirm in writing.
ACTION F126	Assess office resources needed for Stage F and ensure that they are available and adequate.

F130 Client

ACTION F131	Check whether the client has any further comments on the final proposals as developed at the end of Stage E. NOTE *It is not always easy or practical to distinguish final proposals from production information, but there should be no design changes after Stage E, after which any changes made to the brief might cause delay and abortive work. The client should be warned of this. Any alterations that are required should be subject to change control procedures.*
ACTION F132	Check whether the client has confirmed in writing acceptance of the final proposals submitted at Stage E.
ACTION F133	Establish points to be discussed and developed during Stage F.
ACTION F134	Check whether any necessary detail information to be supplied by the client is still outstanding.
ACTION F135	Discuss with the client any outstanding matters of detail design which need to be resolved before preparing production information.

ACTION **F136**	Check whether the client has confirmed in writing the tender procedure to be followed, and whether this is subject to legislative control.
ACTION **F137**	Advise the client on the use of preliminary contracts for enabling works, demolition, etc., if appropriate.
ACTION **F138**	Review with the client the appointment of subcontractors and specialists at this stage and whether it might be advantageous to place advance orders for materials, design or fabrication.
NOTE	*Nomination or naming of subcontractors or suppliers should only be made with the written consent of the client.*
ACTION **F139**	Advise the client on the need for a clerk of works if appropriate, and explain the role of such a person and the appointing procedures. SEE ALSO **J/SM2**
ACTION **F140**	Advise the client on the need for a party wall surveyor, if appropriate.
NOTE	*If the architect is to be appointed as party wall surveyor, this appointment must form a separate agreement.*
ACTION **F141**	Discuss with the client whether interviews with potential contractors should take place at this stage.
NOTE	*Under certain circumstances their views on operational methods and health and safety during construction could be valuable. Contractor involvement can in principle start at any stage. Note comments on how to manage this under previous stages in this book.*
ACTION **F142**	Check with the client when the site will be available to the contractor and that nothing is likely to prevent possession or commencement on that date.
ACTION **F143**	Discuss with the client any intention to impose restrictions on the contractor's working methods (e.g. sequence, access, limitation on hours, noise, etc.).
NOTE	*This could have an effect on production information and would be essential information for tenderers.*

ACTION **F144**	Discuss with the client any proposal for work not forming part of the contract to be carried out by other persons (e.g. the client's own workforce) while the contractor is in possession. Take account of any such confirmed instructions when preparing production information and programming.
ACTION **F145**	Discuss with the client essential information for completing contract documents (e.g. appendix) which will need to be referred to in preliminaries or preambles of bill of quantities/ specification/schedules of work.
ACTION **F146**	Check with the client any special or optional contract provisions.
ACTION **F147**	Check with the client and advisers on insurance for works, etc.

F

F150   Consultant team

ACTION **F151**	Agree the scope of work for each member of the consultant team.
ACTION **F152**	Confirm Stage timetable for services and note its relationship to the project timetable as agreed with the client.
NOTE	*Establish a cut-off point for information to be passed to the cost consultant. This will become information for tenderers. Any subsequent changes are then to be treated formally as contract variations at the appropriate time.*
ACTION **F153**	Confirm arrangements for communication between client, CDMC, project manager and design leader.
ACTION **F154**	Confirm programme and pattern for consultant team meetings.

ACTION F155	Monitor, integrate and coordinate input from consultant team members and specialists. Continue to appraise input from specialist firms, including potential subcontractors and suppliers.
NOTE	*The lead consultant is responsible for facilitating the coordination of all information and its integration into the general scheme.*

ACTION F156	Adopt a formal approach to 'question-and-answer' procedures with the cost consultant as soon as possible.

ACTION F157	Ask the cost consultant to state priorities for receiving information for billing purposes.

ACTION F158	At an early stage, request that all consultant team members use the CPI system for production information if this is practicable.	SEE ALSO **F/SM1** **F/SM2** **F/SM3**

ACTION F159	Continue to cooperate with the CDMC.
	When carrying out design work, avoid foreseeable risks to those involved in the construction and future use of the structure and in so doing eliminate hazards, as far as reasonably practicable, and reduce risk associated with those hazards that remain.
	Provide adequate information about any significant risks associated with the design.
	Coordinate your work with others in order to improve the way that risks are managed and controlled.
	Provide information that other team members are likely to need to identify and manage the remaining risks.
(CONTINUES)	Cooperate with the client and other designers, including those designing temporary works, to ensure that incompatibilities between designs are identified and resolved.

ACTION F159 **CONTINUED**	Cooperation can be encouraged by • setting up an integrated team involving designers, principal contractor and other relevant contractors (once appointed) • the appointment of a lead designer • agreeing a common approach to risk reduction during design • regular meetings of all the design team, including the CDMC, with the contractors and others (once appointed) • regular reviews of the evolving design • site visits, through which designers can gain a direct insight into how the risks are to be managed in practice Review other designers' cooperation with the CDMC with respect to the pre-construction H&S information.
ACTION F160 NOTE	Discuss with the CDMC any outstanding matters of designers' contributions to the pre-construction H&S information. *Remember that the pre-construction H&S information, as prepared by the CDMC, will need to be issued at tender stage.*

F200	**Stage Activities**

F210	**Developing the Production Information**

ACTION F211 (CONTINUES)	Drawings: • Prepare a schedule of drawings and other information needed. • Draw up a programme for the preparation and delivery of the drawings and the other Stage outputs and assess the resource required to complete it in line with the programme.	SEE ALSO **F/SM1**

F

ACTION **F211** CONTINUED	• Confirm a system for recording and distributing information and revisions.
NOTE	*Use standard title panels for all drawings and try to limit the number of different sizes of drawings; A1 is generally the preferred size.* *Compile specification notes as relevant during the production of drawn information.*

ACTION **F212**	Specifications/schedules/bill of quantities:	SEE ALSO **F/SM2** **F/SM3**
	• Agree with the consultant team a strategy including a programme for the production of appropriate documents (e.g. specification/schedules/bill of quantities).	
	• Assemble specification notes made during detail design Stage E.	
	• Prepare a checklist to show which headings or sub-headings might be relevant for the particular project.	
	• Select from the library of standard specification clauses (NBS is recommended).	
	• Mark up a library of clauses and produce a draft copy of the specification.	
	• Identify sections or items that are not covered adequately and which will require special drafting.	
	• Allocate responsibilities for writing particular parts of the specification.	
	• Establish which parts will be by prescription and which by performance requirements.	
	• If specifying by reference, obtain the documents and carefully read the relevant parts.	
	• Review selection of materials, descriptions of workmanship, etc. and check with cost plan.	
	• Decide on the presentation of the specification.	
	• Check final copy for errors, omissions and possible inconsistencies either within parts of the document or between the specification and other production information.	
(CONTINUES)	• Establish the number of copies required and distribute as appropriate.	

ACTION

F212

CONTINUED

NOTE

To assist the cost consultant (QS) during preparation of the bills, the architect might be expected to supply the following:

- *specification or specification notes for incorporation as preambles to work sections*

- *information for inclusion in preliminaries such as:*

  - *form of contract, supplements, option clauses, amended clauses, etc.*
  - *content and use of contract documentation*
  - *method statements required*
  - *pre-tender health and safety information*
  - *work to be done by employer direct*
  - *requirements concerning sequence, time limitations, etc.*
  - *provisional sums to be included*
  - *provision for named/nominated subcontractors/suppliers*

- *diagrams for inclusion in the bills (e.g. extent of retaining structures, cornice profiles, multi-coloured paintwork, etc.)*

Rule 5.3 of SMM refers to the use of dimensioned diagrams in place of a dimensioned description. Drawn information to accompany the bills:

- *location drawings (i.e. block plan, site plan, floor plans, sections and elevations)*

- *component drawings (i.e. showing information necessary for manufacture and assembly)*

- *drawn schedules*

- *dimensions, which will normally appear on the drawings listed above*

In particular, the cost consultant will require overall dimensions, and internal dimensions of all rooms and spaces. Rules 5.1, 5.2 and 5.4 of SMM refer to drawn information. These might be expected to apply to most of the work sections listed above. In many cases this will simply show the scope and location of the work. In other cases (e.g. E, H, etc.) it will require the supply of detail drawings.

The cost consultant will almost certainly expect a rapid response to the query sheets directed at the architect during bill preparations. It will also assist the cost consultant if information is despatched to suit the taking-off process, that is to ensure that the right information is received in the right sequence.

The Standard Method of Measurement contains a full set of the general rules. There is also the SMM Measurement Code published in conjunction with CPI which includes a commentary on particular rules and contains illustrative material likely to be of assistance to the architect.

F

ACTION F213	Obtain the necessary information from firms to be named or nominated.
NOTE	*Obtain this information in good time and place reliance on it only after having secured a design warranty in favour of the client.*
	Check on availability and delivery before including particular materials or sources named in production information.

ACTION F214	Complete the information with respect to prescriptive/performance items in bills, etc.
NOTE	*Take care when including provisional sums that the figure is adequate, and that wherever possible it is for defined work.*

ACTION F215	Draft preliminaries, preambles, specifications for materials and workmanship.
NOTE	*Use specification clauses which are clear and precise. It should be normal practice to use the appropriate version of NBS. It is important that the specification, in addition to the bill of quantities, is incorporated so that it forms part of the contract documentation.*

ACTION F216	Provide information as agreed to the cost consultant for preparation of tender pricing documents (or prepare pricing documents if appointed to do so).

ACTION F217	Consider the requirements for the commissioning of engineering services by subcontractors and the main contractor, and provisions for testing for inclusion in tender documents.

ACTION F218	Prepare report and submit to client.

| NOTE | *If procurement is through design and build:* |

- *for an employer client: check whether the client has confirmed in writing acceptance of proposals and information supplied so far in Stages D–E which are to form part of the Employer's Requirements.*

- *for a contractor client: review any client's comments on the detail design or development and note any adjustments which may be unavoidable owing to modifications introduced lately by component manufacturers or specialist subcontractors.*

Detail design amendments might also be necessary, for example, because of substitutes forced by long delivery times.

Check what action is to be taken as a result.

F

F230	**Inspections/tests**
ACTION F231	Decide on the provisions for testing to be included in the bill of quantities/specification/schedules of work, including contractor's testing and commissioning of building services before completion.
ACTION F232	Determine provisions for the client to witness testing if required and whether this is to be part of the contract period. Establish the contractor's obligations for attendance and rectification if necessary.
ACTION F233	Decide on the method statement required from the appointed contractor on quality management testing, verification, audit and records.
ACTION F234	Review quality management of potential suppliers and subcontractors and their general compliance in health and safety matters. Pass relevant information to the CDMC.

F260	Consultations/approvals/consents

ACTION F261	Check that all necessary information has been obtained with respect to building control approval. Hold further discussions with authorities as necessary to resolve outstanding points.	SEE ALSO **F/SM4**
ACTION F262	If appropriate, continue discussions with the highways authority on matters such as access to site, waiting or off-loading restrictions, siting and design of temporary fencing, hoardings, etc.	
ACTION F263	Discuss, if appropriate, with relevant body (e.g. English Heritage) protective measures for existing works during site operations.	
ACTION F264	Submit Building Notice or application for approval by deposit of Full Plans, if not already submitted, together with relevant documents including a cheque from the client for the appropriate fee.	SEE ALSO **F/SM4**
NOTE	*Compliance can be certified either by the local authority or by an approved inspector. A list of approved inspectors can be obtained from the Construction Industry Council www.cic.org.uk*	
ACTION F265	Check that all party wall and foundation notices have been served.	

F270	Contract

ACTION F271	Agree with the client and the CDMC the tendering period and procedures to be followed in opening tenders and notifying results.
NOTE	*Allow adequate time for tendering, and for the assessment of tenders. The most acceptable tender must be thoroughly checked for errors, and this takes time. Allow time for checking by the CDMC.*

ACTION F272	If necessary, send out preliminary enquiries to firms selected as potential tenderers, as agreed with the client.	SEE ALSO **H/SM1** **H/SM2** **H/SM3** **H/SM4** **H/SM5**

ACTION F273	Arrange interviews to select the principal contractor if relevant and necessary.
NOTE	*Pre-tender meetings and interviews should only be held if considered essential, and always with a strictly limited agenda.*

ACTION F274	If appropriate, arrange for interviews for selection of contractors by negotiation.

ACTION F275	Check that the form of contract to be used has been confirmed with the client in writing.

ACTION F276	Discuss with the client the need to use supplements to cover, for example, sectional completion, contractor's design, fluctuations, etc.

ACTION F277	Discuss with the client the appropriate choice for optional provisions in the contract. Advise on the particulars which need to be entered in the appendix to the contract, and referred to in the tender documents, e.g. dates, insurances, liquidated damages, option clauses, etc.

F

| ACTION F278 | Check, in particular, that the client is aware of the requirements of insurance provisions in the contract and that they appreciate the advisability of seeking specialist advice from their insurers or brokers. |
| NOTE | *It is very important that the client should be fully aware of the insurance requirements well in advance of the tender process.* |

| ACTION F279 | Confirm with the client the inclusion of any special clauses or amendments to the contract, bearing in mind legal advice obtained. |

| ACTION F280 | Review the position with respect to advance orders for design, materials and fabrication by specialist subcontractors and suppliers, including nominated subcontractors. If authorised, take further necessary action. |
| NOTE | *Always obtain authorisation before taking action on advance orders.* |

| ACTION F281 | Confirm with the client any arrangements to employ persons direct to carry out work not forming part of the contract during the contractor's occupation. |

| ACTION F282 | Confirm with the client the details of any preliminary contracts for enabling works and, if authorised, take the necessary action. |

| NOTE | *If procurement is through design and build:* |

- *for an employer client: advise on completion and content of tender documents and the final form and content of the Employer's Requirements.*

- *for a contractor client: inspect drawings and information received from specialist subcontractors and suppliers for checking against contractor's proposals, and advise the client.*

F290	**Cost planning**

ACTION **F291**	Provide information for the cost consultant to review the cost plan and monitor cost implications of decisions during the preparation of production information (or revise the cost estimate if appointed to do so).

ACTION **F292**	Cost consultant (or architect if appointed to do so) to review quotations received from specialist firms and check against provisional sums or budget figures.

NOTE *If procurement is through design and build:*

- *for an employer client: provide revised information if relevant for corrected cost estimates.*

- *for a contractor client: provide revised information if relevant to contractor's estimators.*

F

F300	**General Procedures**

ACTION **F301**	Regularly check progress against the timetable for services (usually monthly).

ACTION **F302**	Continue resource control procedures for the job at regular intervals (usually monthly): • Check expenditure against the office job cost allocation for Stage F. • Monitor fee income against projected fee income.

ACTION **F303**	Report regularly to the client on fees and expenses incurred, and submit accounts at agreed intervals (usually monthly).
NOTE	*Check that the client settles all accounts promptly.*

F400	Stage Outputs

The agreed outputs for Stage F might include the following:

SEE ALSO

F/SM3

- production information coordinated documents – probably including location, component and assembly drawings, drawn schedules, bill of quantities/specification/schedules of work

NOTE *The bill of quantities will normally be produced by the cost consultant.*

- information prepared specially for use in self-build or semi-skilled operations

- information for issue to specialist subcontractors and suppliers in connection with tender invitations

- information for inclusion in pre-construction H&S information to be passed to the CDMC

- information which is not necessarily part of the tender package for use in dealings with third parties, landlords, tenants, funders, etc. (e.g. in connection with leases, boundaries, party walls, etc.)

NOTE *If procurement is through design and build:*

- *for an employer client: detail design information for incorporation into Employer's Requirements (part of Stages D–G).*

- *for a contractor client: general arrangement drawings, interface details, performance specification and other technical information (part of Stages F–G).*

Supplementary Material

F/SM1: Production information drawings

Coordinated Project Information

Many problems and delays on site are due to inaccurate or incomplete information, and it is essential that the tender drawings, specifications, etc., and any subsequent production information produced, is complete and fully coordinated.

The use of Coordinated Project Information (CPI) is recommended for all projects regardless of procurement method. The Construction Project Information Committee (CPIC), a body made up of representatives of RIBA, RICS, ICE, CIBSE and the Construction Confederation, has been responsible for providing best practice guidance on the content, form and preparation of construction production information and making sure this best practice is disseminated throughout the UK construction industry. The CPIC publication *Production Drawings: A Code of Procedure for the Construction Industry* can be found on the CPIC website at www.productioninformation.org and provides best practice advice for this aspect of the procurement process.

The importance of non-adversarial team working has long been recognised. Current IT technology facilitates such tools as the single project model that rely on an integrated team structure, and good information is essential in maintaining a non-adversarial environment and a successful project.

Structure of drawings

G/SM1 sets out how production information drawings should comprise location drawings, component drawings and dimensioned diagrams in accordance with SMM.

Drawings from the structural engineer and the building services engineers should be structured in a compatible manner despite the fact that information in their cases is likely to come from a number of sources, including specialist subcontractors and suppliers.

Purpose of drawings

Drawings at this Stage are produced for three main reasons:

- because they must accompany bill of quantities or other tendering documentation and generally as stipulated by SMM
- because they will later become contract documents

F

- because they may need to be developed or issued as other 'necessary information' under the building contract to the main contractor when work on site commences

The number of drawings required is likely to be influenced by the size of the project, the procurement method to be adopted (i.e. who actually produces the drawings), and the relative significance of drawn information in relation to other contract documents.

Whatever drawings are produced it is important to be clear about their intended purpose and the needs of the user of the drawing. Any drawing should provide such information as shape or profile, dimensions (notional or finished), position, composition and relation to other parts including tolerances, fixing methods, etc. On a small project where only a small number of drawings is necessary, these might embrace the needs of all trades and suppliers and be annotated to the extent that no other supporting document is required.

Conversely, larger projects will require a considerable number of drawings and schedules, each devised with a particular trade or element in mind, and cross-referencing to other drawings will need to be carried out with great care.

A checklist of the parts of a building that may need to be covered in a production information drawing and schedule programme is given in Fig. E4.

Schedules

Some information is more clearly and conveniently conveyed in schedule form. This has traditionally been in drawn form, on A1 sheets for example, but is now more commonly produced as an electronic spreadsheet. Schedules commonly include:

- ironmongery (with location and fixings)
- doors
- windows (to include glazing)
- finishes (floor, walls, ceilings)
- precast lintels and sills
- inspection chambers and manhole covers
- colours

Any elements or components which are repetitive or can be grouped may be suitable for scheduling. The exercise is a good coverage check for compilers but information should not be repeated on the drawings as this might lead to confusion and inconsistencies.

It is quite common for suppliers to provide schedules on the architect's behalf but these should be thoroughly checked.

F/SM2: Specification and schedules of work

CPI procedures

The introduction of Coordinated Project Information (CPI) procedures has created an efficient way of achieving integrated architectural and engineering drawings, specifications and bills of quantities. The Common Arrangement of Work Sections for building works (CAWS) has been adopted throughout the documents. CAWS is the result of detailed analysis of UK subcontracting practice and is compiled at the level of 'minimum subcontract package' termed 'work sections'. There should never be a need for further sub-division but it is normal to aggregate a number of work sections when letting actual subcontract packages. The National Building Specification (NBS), National Engineering Specification (NES) and Standard Method of Measurement (SMM) all use this arrangement. The architect and the cost consultant will find it easier to prepare and interpret a specification where it shares a common arrangement with the method of measurement used in preparing the bills and it also facilitates better understanding of the documents by contractors and specialists.

The specification

It is vital to understand that long before a specification evolves into a written document it is a process completely integrated with design. It eventually becomes a written document which may describe the materials or products to be used, standards of workmanship required, performance requirements and the conditions under which the work will be carried out. It should be clearly and economically worded, with the objective of transferring information from designers to constructors with accuracy and certainty.

A specification can be prescriptive, in that there is precise description of the materials, workmanship, etc. which leaves no area of choice to the tendering contractor. It can also be written as performance requirements either for the building components or for engineering services, in which case there will remain an area of choice on the part of the contractor as to how the stated performance will be achieved. If performance specification is to be used, great care needs to be taken in ensuring that the contractual terms recognise this additional responsibility of the contractor. In reality most modern specification sections use a combination of performance and prescription.

Some architects' practices might use a system of specification clauses developed for use with particular types of work (e.g. housing refurbishment). Care must be taken to keep such clauses relevant and up to date, and it is generally safer and more convenient to adopt a well-developed system such as NBS. This allows

F

for consistent description of materials and workmanship with full reference to British Standards and other codes and standards. NBS also enables performance specifications to be developed.

NBS is available in electronic form as 'NBS Building' (refer to www.thenbs.com) an easy-to-use software package that enables the development of specifications on screen, referring to guidance and other technical information such as British Standards. Some clauses require additional information that can be typed in or completed by using drop-down lists of suggested solutions.

Under CPI the specification is the core document to which the other production information refers. The description of materials and workmanship contained in the specification should therefore not be repeated on the drawing or in the bills – these documents should refer to clause numbers in the specification. A specification will therefore be needed even when there is a separate bill of quantities. CPI advocates giving it contract document status by, for example, making it part of the bills. This can be done by calling the specification 'Bill Number 2'. Alternatively it can be done by including the specification at the start of the bills, or by introducing the relevant parts of the specification as preambles to the various measured work sections of the bill of quantities.

Where there is no bill of quantities, it may be wise to append a schedule of work to the specification for pricing purposes, possibly supported by a schedule of rates, or to require the tendering contractor to provide a priced activity schedule. If the specification has been prepared using the CAWS system then a breakdown according to work sections may not be very helpful when it comes to valuing variations or certificates.

The architect as designer is responsible for the method of specification selected, and the content. Specification notes will normally be compiled during the design process. The specification is a key document and will provide information to:

- the cost consultant when preparing bills of quantities
- the contractor's estimator when preparing a tender
- the clerk of works and the contractor during construction work

Members of the design team might prepare the specification for those parts of the work which require specialist knowledge but the architect as design team leader should coordinate overall content.

Schedules of work

Schedules of work comprise lists of the various items of work to be carried out, usually on a room-by-room basis. It is customary to introduce a number or area alongside the items to encourage systematic pricing by tenderers. Items in respect of each room are usually listed under headings such as doors, ceilings, wall finishes, floor finishes, fittings, etc. Schedules of work should not contain quantities, for they are not exact documents by nature. A contractor, when pricing, should be expected to include everything necessary to complete the works.

Schedules of work might be contract documents where there is no bill of quantities. They are sometimes regarded as an alternative to a specification, particularly when used for housing refurbishment or alteration work. However, CPI would recommend that the specification is used, and that the items in the schedule of work refer to the detailed descriptions in the specification.

F

F/SM3: Bill of quantities

Pricing a bill of quantities is the traditional method of obtaining comparable tenders for projects where the design has been fully detailed beforehand. Where an accurate or full bill of quantities becomes part of the contract documentation, it usually means that quality and quantity included in the price will be as stated in the contract bills. It is therefore important to ensure that the bill accurately reflects the intentions of the architect and does not conflict with information shown on the drawings.

Notional bill or approximate quantities

Where it is not possible to present the cost consultant with a completely detailed design and specification, it may be possible to invite tenders on the basis of notional bill or approximate quantities. These should be reasonably accurate as to description and items, with only the amounts left subject to measurement after completion.

Work which cannot be quantified with certainty, even in an accurate bill of quantities, may be covered by the introduction of provisional sums (for either defined or undefined work), prime cost sums (where an accurate figure can be placed on a subcontract or supply item), or an approximate quantity (where the item is certain but the quantity is not).

The inclusion of a contingency sum is nothing more than a provisional figure for undefined work of an unforeseeable nature. All such items require later instructions from the architect before the contractor can act on them.

Standard Method of Measurement

A uniform basis of measuring work for inclusion in a bill of quantities may be found in the *Standard Method of Measurement of Building Works*, currently in a seventh edition (SMM7). For building work this is most likely to be using the Common Arrangement and in accordance with SMM. The contents of a bill prepared in this way are likely to include:

- Preliminaries/general conditions
- items which are not specific to work sections but which have an identifiable cost (e.g. site facilities, insurances)
- items for fixed and time-related costs (e.g. plant, temporary works)

Work sections (also incorporating cross-references to drawings and specification)

    C Demolition/alteration/renovation

D   Groundwork
E   In situ concrete/large precast concrete
F   Masonry – brick, block, stonework, etc.
G   Structural/carcassing – metal and timber
H   Cladding/covering – patent glazing, plastics, etc.
J   Waterproofing
K   Linings/dry partitions
L   Windows/doors/stairs
M   Surface finishes – screeds, tiling, decorating, etc.
P   Building fabric sundries – trims, ironmongery, etc.
Q   Paving/planting/fencing/outdoor furniture
R   Disposal systems – pipework gutters, drainage
Y   Mechanical and electrical services

For a comprehensive schedule of drawings required refer to the CPIC publication *Production: A Code of Procedure for the Construction Industry*, Appendix DE, which can be found at www.productioninformation.org.

F

F/SM4: Building control approval

Preparing an application for Building Regulations approval is normally one of the services provided by the architect. In many cases, although informal consultations may well have taken place earlier, the drawings and calculations necessary to support a formal submission will not be sufficiently developed until well into production information.

The government website www.planningportal.gov.uk provides a clear explanation of all the current regulations and the procedures for making applications for approval. This site includes sections on such matters as water efficiency, the 'Code for Sustainable Homes', the legislation that governs the Regulations, technical guidance on all the Approved Documents, the approval process, determination and appeals, a list of useful contacts and links to related internet sites.

Another useful website is www.communities.gov.uk. This contains information on 'Home Information Packs' and 'Energy Performance Certificates', the White Paper 'Planning for a Sustainable Future', the new fire safety laws, and many other relevant matters. It also contains the 'Building Regulations Explanatory Booklet', which provides a general guide to making an application.

In 2007 there were significant changes to Approved Document L 'Conservation of Fuel and Power'. In particular, it is important to note the requirement to submit energy performance calculations on completion of construction work, which must be performed by a certified person.

Regard should also be had to the Disability Discrimination Act 1995, a copy of which can be found at www.opsi.gov.uk

Tender Documentation

As defined in *RIBA Outline Plan of Work 2007*:

■ Preparation and/or collation of tender documentation in sufficient detail to enable a tender or tenders to be obtained for the project*

* These activities may be moved to suit project requirements

CONTENTS

G

Stage Description

Generally Stage G involves the assembly and coordination of all the production information into the tender package. In addition, it is the Stage when the final cost plan is prepared by the cost consultant. This is an essential final check – before proceeding to tender – that the design as currently developed still meets the client's budget. It should be noted, however, that the cost plan should be updated regularly throughout the design process, with increasing levels of predictive accuracy. If the estimate reveals any unanticipated problems then some adjustment of the production information may be needed, before going out to tender. If this is the case it will require careful management and collaboration from all concerned.

Design and build procurement

In design and build procurement, Stage G (and H) may be out of sequence with the other Work Stages. In cases where the client wishes to tender on detailed information the stages may follow something close to the normal sequence, but in others, where the design and build contract is entered into on minimal information, Stage G may follow Stage C, with Stages D–F occurring after the contract is let and sometimes during construction.

Management procurement

With management procurement, the amount of production information available at the commencement of the project will be limited to the extent that much detail information will be supplied by the works contractors by way of shop or installation drawings. Nevertheless, the general production information will originate from the professional team, and the process of coordinating and integrating information will continue throughout the construction of the project.

G

Key Obligations

(from RIBA Agreements 2007: Standard Agreements (S-Con-07): Schedule of Design Services (SS-DS-07))

Provide information for preparation of tender pricing documents OR

Prepare schedules of rates/schedules of works for tendering purposes.

Prepare and collate tender documents to enable a tender or tenders to be obtained.

Assist lead consultant to identify and evaluate potential tenderers.

Provide information for preparation of pre-tender estimate of relevant cost.

Prepare and submit to client a Stage G report.

G100	**Preliminary Issues**

G110	**Information required**

Check that all information necessary during Stage G is available:

- production information prepared during Stage F

- any further conditions imposed by the local building control and fire authorities, particularly relating to construction details and fire prevention, including finishes

NOTE *See note under this section in Stage F re the Regulatory Reform (Fire Safety) Order 2005.*

- further contributions, information and recommendations from consultants in relation to documents submitted by approved subcontractors and suppliers

G

G120	**Appointment**

ACTION **G121**   Establish scope, content and context for Stage G activities.

NOTE *Put it into context, particularly if previous stages were undertaken by others. If possible, establish whether material produced now is likely to be acted upon by others taking over subsequent Stages.*

ACTION **G122**	If coming new to the project at this Stage in the Plan of Work: • Ascertain that relevant Pre-Agreement and earlier Stage checks have been carried out. • Agree fees and timetable with the client.
NOTE	*Allow for familiarisation and reviewing of all usable material.* • Confirm the role of the architect in relation to the rest of the consultant team. • Ensure that you have the necessary competency and resource to undertake the design work and address the H&S issues likely to be involved in it. • Request a copy of the project-specific, pre-construction health and safety information and review it. • Advise the client of their responsibilities under the CDM Regulations and ensure that a CDMC has been appointed.
NOTE	*Where a project is notifiable, the regulations require that the client appoints a CDMC as soon as is practicable after initial design work or other preparation for construction work has begun. This would generally be at Stage C.* • Ensure that you have adequate professional indemnity insurance cover.
ACTION **G123**	Check that the client's instruction to proceed has been given and confirmed in writing.
ACTION **G124**	Check that the client has settled all accounts submitted to date.
ACTION **G125**	Check appointing documents with respect to services and fees: • If the services, cost or time targets are different from the agreement with the client, agree a formal variation by letter or deed as appropriate. • If the extent of professional services for Stage G is not settled, agree with the client and confirm in writing. • If the methods and levels of charging for Stage G are not yet settled, agree with the client and confirm in writing.
ACTION **G126**	Assess office resources needed for Stage G and ensure that they are available and adequate.

G130	Client
ACTION **G131**	Check whether the client has confirmed in writing acceptance of any proposals and information submitted at Stage F.
ACTION **G132**	Establish any points to be discussed and developed during Stage G.
ACTION **G133**	Check whether any necessary contractual information to be supplied by the client is still outstanding.
ACTION **G134**	Confirm with the client the details of any preliminary contracts for enabling works, demolition, etc.
ACTION **G135**	Confirm with the client the details of any advance appointments of subcontractors and specialists. Ensure that the client has copies of relevant warranties.
ACTION **G136**	Confirm with the client the details of any clerk of works' appointments if appropriate. SEE ALSO **J/SM2**
ACTION **G137**	Arrange with the client for further interviews of potential contractors if appropriate.
ACTION **G138**	Confirm with the client the details of any phasing, restrictions and implications.
ACTION **G139**	Confirm with the client the details of any proposal for work not forming part of the contract to be carried out by other persons.
ACTION **G140**	Confirm with the client the list of tenderers.
ACTION **G141**	Confirm with the client the details of contract appendix entries.
ACTION **G142**	Confirm with the client the details of any special or optional contract provisions.
ACTION **G143**	Confirm with the client and advisers that arrangements for insurance for works, etc. are being made.

G

G150	Consultant team
ACTION G151	Agree input to the Stage by consultant team members.
ACTION G152	Confirm Stage timetable for services and note its relationship to the project timetable as agreed with the client.
ACTION G153	Confirm timetable for receipt of any revisions to tender information required from consultant team members.
NOTE	*Establish a cut-off point for revised information to be passed to the cost consultant.*
ACTION G154	Confirm patterns for communication between the client, CDMC, project manager and design leader.
ACTION G155	Confirm programme and pattern for consultant team meetings.
ACTION G156	Integrate and coordinate input from consultant team members and specialists if this is covered under the architect's conditions of appointment.
ACTION G157	Continue to appraise input from specialist firms, including potential subcontractors and suppliers.
ACTION G158	Provide final information for pre-construction H&S information and pass to the CDMC.
ACTION G159	Discuss with the CDMC any outstanding matters of designers' contributions to the pre-construction H&S information.
ACTION G160	Coordinate production of the Information Release Schedule if appropriate.
ACTION G161	Confirm with consultant team members any further arrangements for inviting specialist tenders.
ACTION G162	Continue to appraise input from specialist firms, including potential subcontractors and suppliers.

G200	Stage Activities

G210	**Preparing the tender documents**

ACTION G211	Obtain from subcontractors and suppliers any outstanding project information.
ACTION G212	Provide final information to the cost consultant for bills and the pre-tender cost estimate.
ACTION G213	Consolidate the final detailed information for production drawings, subcontract specifications and preliminaries to bills of quantities/specification/schedules of work.
ACTION G214	Establish the form of the building contract and its conditions.
ACTION G215	Prepare, coordinate, collate and check tender documents.
ACTION G216	Prepare report and submit to the client.
ACTION G217	Request authority of the client to invite tenders.

NOTE

If procurement is through design and build:

- *for an employer client: check whether the client has confirmed in writing acceptance of proposals and information supplied so far in Stages D–G which are to form part of the Employer's Requirements.*

- *for a contractor client: review any client comments on the detail design or development, and note any adjustments which may be unavoidable owing to modifications introduced recently by component manufacturers or specialist subcontractors.*

Detail design amendments might also be necessary, for example, because of substitutes forced by long delivery times.

Check what action is to be taken as a result.

G260	Approvals/consents

ACTION G261	Monitor progress on statutory and other consents. Submit additional information if necessary.

ACTION G262	Monitor progress on party wall awards.

G270	Contract

ACTION G271	Confirm any outstanding details of the contractual terms – including supplements, optional provisions, particulars – which need to be entered in the appendix to the contract.	
ACTION G272	Discuss with the client the results of any pre-selection interviews or other selection procedures, and take any necessary further action.	SEE ALSO **H/SM1**
ACTION G273	Confirm with the client the final tender list, and inform all tenderers of their inclusion.	
ACTION G274	Check that the client has finalised all insurance arrangements.	
ACTION G275	Check that all advance orders for design, materials and fabrication by specialist subcontractors and suppliers, as agreed, have been placed.	
ACTION G276	Check that any preliminary contracts for enabling works are under way and on schedule. Administer the preliminary contracts, if authorised.	
ACTION G277	If appropriate, confirm with the client that the appointment of a clerk of works is in hand.	

ACTION **G278**	Confirm with the client that any arrangements to employ persons direct to carry out work not forming part of the contract are in hand.

ACTION **G279**	Review, with other consultant team members, any further tenders received from specialist subcontractors and suppliers. Include in tender documents as appropriate.

> **NOTE** *If procurement is through design and build:*
>
> - *for an employer client: advise on completion and content of tender documents and the final form and content of the Employer's Requirements.*
>
> - *for a contractor client: inspect drawings and information received from specialist subcontractors and suppliers for checking against contractor's proposals, and advise the client.*

G290	**Cost planning**

ACTION **G291** **NOTE**	Provide information for the cost consultant to prepare a pre-tender cost estimate (or prepare pre-tender cost estimate if appointed to do so). *The pre-tender estimate is an essential check prior to inviting tenders. At this point the estimate should be an accurate prediction of the tender figures. The design and tender documents may need to be amended if the estimate does not match the project brief.*

ACTION **G292**	Review with the client the implications of the pre-tender estimate prepared by the cost consultant.

ACTION **G293**	Discuss possible options with the client. Explain implications for timetable and consultants' fees if amendments are required to change (or comply with) the brief.

ACTION G294	Report to the client on cost matters at agreed intervals.

NOTE	*If procurement is through design and build:*
	• *for an employer client: provide revised information if relevant for corrected cost estimates.*
	• *for a contractor client: provide revised information if relevant to contractor's estimators.*

G300 General Procedures

ACTION G301	Regularly check progress against the timetable for services.

ACTION G302	Continue resource control procedures for the job (usually monthly):
	• Check expenditure against the office job cost allocation for Stage G.
	• Monitor fee income against the projected fee income.

ACTION G303	Report regularly to the client on fees and expenses incurred and submit accounts at agreed intervals (usually monthly).
NOTE	*Check that the client settles all accounts promptly.*

G400	Stage Outputs

Check that all the agreed outputs have been produced, which might include the following:

SEE ALSO
F/SM1
F/SM2
F/SM3
G/SM1

- finalised tender documents – probably including drawings, schedules, bills of quantities/specification/schedules of work, pre-construction H&S information, terms of bonds and warranties, subcontractor information and tenders. When sending out for tender, any of the following documents and information may be relevant:

  - a list of all tender documents so that the tenderers can check they have received the complete package
  - tender forms and details of procedure to be followed, e.g. type of tender required, submittals required, how the tender should be packaged and identified, to whom it should be sent
  - site information and surveys
  - drawings
  - drawn schedules, e.g. for doors
  - specification
  - bill of quantities
  - list of items to be paid for prior to delivery on site
  - schedule of works
  - schedule of rates
  - activity schedule
  - Information Release Schedule
  - the Health and Safety Plan
  - programmed dates for proposed work
  - details of any phased commencement or completion
  - details of the contract terms and conditions, including insurance provisions
  - details of advance payment arrangements
  - details of any bonds or guarantees required from the contractor or to be provided by the employer
  - details of any warranties to be provided

NOTE

Refer to G/SM1 for a comprehensive schedule of information to be provided.

(CONTINUES)

G

CONTINUED	• information prepared specially for use in self-build or semi-skilled operations	SEE ALSO **F/SM1**
	• information for issue to specialist subcontractors and suppliers in connection with tender invitations	**F/SM2** **F/SM3** **G/SM1**
	• information which is not necessarily part of the tender package for use in dealings with third parties, landlords, tenants, funders, etc. (e.g. in connection with leases, boundaries, party walls, etc.)	

NOTE   *If procurement is through design and build:*

• *for an employer client: detail design information for incorporation into Employer's Requirements (part of Stages D–G).*

• *for a contractor client: general arrangement drawings, interface details, performance specification and other technical information (part of Stages F–G).*

Supplementary Material

G/SM1: Tender documentation checklist

NOTE *There is a separate list for Employer's Requirements at G/SM2.*

The CPIC Production Information Code gives guidance on drawn information to be issued to tenderers. It covers contracts with and without quantities, sets out the definitions and rules relating to drawn information in the *Standard Method of Measurement of Building Works* (SMM7) and gives guidance on how those requirements may be satisfied.

Prior to tender Stage drawn information is used mainly for the measurement of quantities. On 'with quantities' contracts SMM requires drawn information to be provided to tenderers to give:

- an overall picture of the project to allow assessment of the cost significance of the design and decisions to be made about methods of construction
- detailed information about parts of the work where this information is more effectively communicated graphically than by a lengthy description in the bill of quantities

The requirements for provision of this information are dealt with below. Drawings selected from those normally available for construction of the project should satisfy the SMM requirements (except for dimensioned diagrams).

Apart from the specific requirements for provision of drawings, SMM allows descriptive and specification information to be given on drawings or in the specification, provided a specific cross-reference is given in the bill of quantities description of the item (SMM General Rule 4.2).

The following types of drawings are referred to in SMM:

- location drawings
- component drawings
- dimensioned diagrams

Location drawings

The SMM rules for Preliminaries/General conditions require certain location drawings to accompany the bill of quantities. These are defined in General Rule 5.1 as follows:

(a) Block Plan: shall identify the site and locate the outlines of the building works in relation to a town plan or other context.

G

(b) Site Plan: shall locate the position of the building works in relation to setting out points, means of access and general layout of the site.

(c) Plans, Sections and Elevations: shall show the position occupied by the various spaces in a building and the general construction and location of principal elements.

The architect's smaller scale location drawings will normally satisfy this requirement. The majority of work sections in SMM commence with a statement of the information to be provided specifically for that type of work. The requirements will normally be met by the architect's location drawings referred to above. If not, other drawings produced by the architect, structural, mechanical and electrical engineers, etc. should be provided.

SMM7 applies equally to all with quantities projects. However, when deciding which drawings to include to comply with the rules, the type, size and relative complexity of the particular project will need to be considered. For example the scope and location of foul drainage above ground for a simple single storey building may be adequately defined by the general arrangement floor plan showing the sanitary appliances whereas more detailed drawn information will be required for this work in a more complex building.

In addition to the requirements concerning location drawings there are other SMM rules, which although not specifically referring to drawings, can often be complied with to best advantage by giving information on drawings referenced from the bills of quantities. An example is Section D20 Excavating and filling which requires details of:

- ground water level
- trial pits or bore hole details stating their location
- features retained
- live over or underground services indicating location

Component drawings

Component drawings are required by General Rule 5.2 to show the information necessary for the manufacture and assembly of components.

Dimensioned diagrams

Dimensioned diagrams are required by SMM General Rule 5.3 to show the shape and dimensions of the work covered by an item. They may be used at the discretion of the quantity surveyor as an alternative to a dimensioned description except in those cases where there is a specific requirement for a dimensioned diagram. Dimensioned diagrams may be prepared by the quantity surveyor or, on their behalf, by the architect. They can also be extracts from the architect's or engineer's drawings reproduced at a suitable size for incorporation in the bills of quantities.

Dimensioned diagrams should not appear in documentation other than the bills of quantities. However, there may be occasions where it is more appropriate to issue the architect's or engineer's drawings with the bills of quantities rather than produce dimensioned diagrams. In such instances it will be necessary to identify the drawings in the bill description.

Preparation of tender documents

The tender documentation will include the bills of quantities, the tender drawings, the project specification (as appropriate), the form of tender and the letter of invitation. The bills of quantities will list the drawings from which the bills have been prepared, and copies of these should be kept as a record. It is good practice to indicate which of the drawings listed accompany the tender documents.

As much of the drawn information as possible should be contained within the bills of quantities to minimise the problem of expensive reproduction of drawings. The provision of copy negatives or similar methods rather than prints will also assist in keeping down tendering costs.

It will be of assistance to contractors if, when domestic subcontractors are named in bills of quantities, the drawings and the specification relevant to their work are sent to them direct, obviating the need for all tendering contractors to do so when they can see from the bill that this has been done.

Refer to F/SM3 for a schedule of location drawings required.

G

G/SM2: Design and build documentation

Employer's Requirements

The Employer's Requirement document is the basis for obtaining tenders and is created during the Pre-Construction Work Stages C–G (or such other stages as may be agreed for the project) prior to inviting tenders at Stage H. It might comprise:

Preliminaries and contract conditions:

> JCT DB05 Schedule 2 Supplemental Provisions
>
> 1. Named subcontractors
> 2. Bills of quantities
> 3. Valuation of change instructions
> 4. Direct loss and/or expense
>
> Pre-construction information pack

Design information
(all or part may be by way of performance specification)

> 1:100 plans, sections and elevations
> 1:500 site layout, including critical setting out data
> 1:50 room layout plans
> Site – extent, external works and access
> Landscape design
> Fire compartments and escape routes
> Engineering services mains and risers
> Plant spaces
> Drainage – main runs
> Enabling works

Specification

> Quality – aesthetics
> Constraints
> Materials and workmanship
> Technical standards
> Building owner's manual – operation and maintenance
> Health and Safety File

Schedules

> Equipment including sanitary and storage fittings, user outlets, etc.
> Commissioning and testing

Other information

> Brief
> Client's health and safety policy
> Site constraints (covenants etc.)
> Topographical surveys
> Geotechnical report
> Existing engineering services and/or main supplies
> Planning consent – outline/detailed/reserved matters
> Statutory consultation records
> Room data sheets

The amount of information to be included in the Employer's Requirements can vary enormously. A straightforward project requiring a relatively simple design solution which can be left largely to the contractor may need little more than basic details of site and accommodation. With a more complex problem, or a design which needs sensitivity of detail, the Employer's Requirements might extend to a full scheme design.

The number and detail of documents that make up the Employer's Requirements will be influenced by considerations such as:

- how much design control the employer wishes to retain, for example in the interests of maintenance programmes or because of functional requirements
- whether the employer regards the process as more of a develop and construct operation, where only constructional details are left in the hands of the contractor
- whether contractor's standard unit types will form the basis of the scheme
- whether the employer will require design continuity via novation or a 'consultant switch'
- whether the employer has appointed a planning supervisor and whether the pre-tender Health and Safety Plan exists

Generally the Requirements will always need to include basic information, such as the following:

- site information and requirements (e.g. boundaries, topography, known subsoil conditions, existing services)
- site constraints (e.g. limitations of access, storage) and relevant easements or restrictive covenants
- topographical surveys
- geotechnical reports
- planning permission obtained or conditions known (contractors will not usually tender until outline planning permission has been obtained)

G

- reports on other statutory consultations
- existing Health and Safety Files, client's health and safety policy documents
- functional nature of the building(s) (e.g. kind and number of units) and accommodation requirements
- schematic layout of the building (or more developed design as appropriate)
- specific requirements as to forms of construction, materials, services, finishes, equipment, etc.
- specification information, probably including performance specifications
- room data sheets
- equipment and fitting schedules
- details of special programming requirements (e.g. phased completion)
- contract data or special requirements (e.g. named subcontractors, as built information)
- requirements concerning contractor's design liability, insurance cover, design team, requirement to use employer's designers, etc.
- clear statement of the extent of information and detail to be included in the contractor's proposals
- content and form of the contract sum analysis
- if JCT DB05 is to be used, information related to supplementary provisions

It is generally accepted that too specific an approach over design and constructional matters, or the specifying of proprietary systems and materials, may reduce the contractor's design liability in the event of a failure.

Contractor's Proposals

These will be in direct response to the Employer's Requirements. Architects acting as consultants to a contractor client will first need to check the information provided to establish whether it is adequate. A query list is often necessary to obtain clarification on matters of conflict or omission.

Submissions sometimes take the form of an A3 brochure, and typically include the following:

- design drawings (e.g. site layout, floor plans, elevations, principal sections, some detailed drawings, landscaping)
- structural details (e.g. foundation and structure general arrangement drawings)
- mechanical services (e.g. layouts of ducts, pipe runs, schematic indications for all systems)
- electrical services (e.g. floor layouts showing lighting, power, alarms)
- specifications (e.g. particular for trades prescription and performance, general specification for workmanship, materials, finishes)
- programme (e.g. bar chart)

- method statements (e.g. general organisational matters and in particular the health and safety information proposals)

The tender figure will usually be required to be made separately. With it will be the contract sum analysis.

The structure of the contract sum analysis will be in accordance with the Employer's Requirements. A typical breakdown could be:

- design work
- preliminaries
- health and safety provisions
- demolition
- excavation
- concrete
- brickwork and blockwork
- roofing and cladding
- woodwork
- structural steelwork
- metalwork
- mechanical and plumbing services
- electrical services
- glazing
- painting and decorating
- drainage and external works

G

As defined in *RIBA Outline Plan of Work 2007*:

- ■ Identification and evaluation of potential contractors and/or specialists for the project*
- ■ Obtaining and appraising tenders; submission of recommendations to the client*

  * These activities may be moved to suit project requirements

CONTENTS

Stage Description

Tendering is an activity not wholly confined to Stage H. For example, there will often be the need to obtain tenders from specialist subcontractors or suppliers at an earlier Stage. Sometimes it may be advantageous if the main contractor is appointed earlier to advise pre-construction, followed by a second stage tender for the full contract works. Obviously the procurement method adopted – or the size and complexity of the project – can have an effect on Tender Action and timing. For example, in management procurement, there will be a tendering procedure to select the management contractor (or construction manager) followed by separate tendering for each works package. Normally, however, Stage H is when the main contract tenders are invited and evaluated, and advice is given to the client on appointing the contractor.

Tenders may be obtained by following one of these routes:

- open tendering – open to all and in theory competitive but generally regarded as wasteful, often unreliable, and not in the client's long-term interests
- selective tendering – open to selected invitees only, competitive and appropriate for all forms of procurement but with fair and clear criteria for selection
- negotiated tendering – applicable where price is not the main criterion, and not necessarily competitive except perhaps where it forms the second step in a two-stage process – this may not be applicable for certain public sector contracts (e.g. EU procurement rules)

Tendering will mostly be a single-stage activity but where the project is particularly large and complex, or where the procurement method makes it desirable, two-stage tendering can be a more efficient and satisfactory way forward.

Regardless of the route chosen, it is important to ensure that tendering is always on a fair basis. Competition should only be between firms who have the necessary skills, integrity, responsibility and reputation to enable them to deliver work of the nature and standard required. Competitive tendering should involve only a realistic number of bids from firms who have been given the same information and the same realistic period in which to formulate offers.

It is sound practice always to follow current relevant guidance.

Tendering in the local or public authority sectors may also be subject to standing orders, and the Public Contracts Regulations 2006 and any subsequent legislation. Where such legislation applies it is important that it is followed exactly.

H

Key Obligations

(from RIBA Agreements 2007: Standard Agreements (S-Con-07): Schedule of Design Services (SS-DS-07))

Contribute to appraisal and report on tenders/negotiations.

If instructed, revise construction information to match adjustments in the tender sum.

H100	Preliminary Issues

H110	Information required

Check that all information necessary during Stage H is available:

- tender documents, complete and ready for dispatch to invited tenderers

- pre-construction H&S information

- tender list as agreed with client

- completed tender documents from nominated or named subcontractors and suppliers with all sections properly completed

- relevant published procedure notes and guidance on selected method of tendering (e.g. Construction Industry Board publications available through the Constrauction Industry Council website, www.cic.org.uk, JCT Practice Note 6 Series 2))

- completed particulars for contract, and for supplements to form of contract

- pre-tender cost estimate prepared by cost consultant based on bills of quantities/specification/schedules of work

H

H120   Appointment

| ACTION H121 | Establish scope, content and context for Stage H activities. |

NOTE
Put it into context, particularly if previous stages were undertaken by others. If possible, establish whether material produced now is likely to be acted upon by others taking over subsequent Stages.

If the appointment includes Stage L2, the architect must contribute to appraisal of tenders/negotiations relative to occupation strategies and facilities management matters.

If the appointment includes Stage L3, the architect must identify any changes to targets and their causes.

| ACTION H122 | If coming new to the project at this stage in the Plan of Work: |

- Ascertain that Pre-Agreement and earlier stage checks have been carried out.

- Agree fees and timetable with the client.

NOTE
Allow for familiarisation and reviewing of all usable material.

- Confirm the role of the architect in relation to the rest of the consultant team.

- Ensure that you have the necessary competency and resource to undertake the design work and address the H&S issues likely to be involved in it.

- Request a copy of the project-specific, pre-construction health and safety information and review it.

- Advise the client of their responsibilities under the CDM Regulations and ensure that a CDMC has been appointed.

NOTE
Where a project is notifiable, the regulations require that the client appoints a CDMC as soon as is practicable after initial design work or other preparation for construction work has begun. This would generally be at Stage C.

- Ensure that you have adequate professional indemnity insurance cover.

ACTION **H123**	Check that the client's instruction to proceed has been given and request that this is confirmed in writing.
ACTION **H124**	Check that the client has settled all accounts submitted to date.
ACTION **H125**	Check appointing documents with respect to services and fees: • If the services, cost or time targets are different from the agreement with the client, agree a formal variation by letter or deed, as appropriate. • If the extent of professional services for Stage H is not yet settled, agree with the client and confirm in writing. • If the methods and levels of charging for Stage H are not yet settled, agree with the client and confirm in writing.
ACTION **H126**	Assess the office resources needed for Stage H and ensure that they are available and adequate. Agree the arrangement for any additional services in case of design changes or tender renegotiation to meet the cost plan.

H130 | Client

ACTION **H131**	Check whether the client has confirmed the following: • whether tendering for the particular project is subject to legislative control • the preferred tendering method, any client tender operational requirements and the method for selecting names to be included on the tender list
ACTION **H132**	Clarify and confirm any outstanding matters related to the tendering procedure to be followed in writing, including procedures to be followed after receipt of tenders.

H

ACTION
H133
Check with the client that the site will be available to the contractor on the date stated in the documents, and that there is nothing likely to prevent possession or commencement.

H150   Consultant team

ACTION
H151
Agree timetable and input to the stage by consultant team members.

ACTION
H152
Confirm programme and pattern for any further meetings of the consultant team.

ACTION
H153
Check with consultant team members their input to main contract tender documents to discover inconsistencies or omissions.

ACTION
H154
Review with consultant team members tenders and accompanying information received from specialist subcontractors and suppliers and, if acceptable, approve them.

H200   Stage Activities

H210   Sending out for tenders

ACTION
H211
Make a final check of information for main contract tenders, including:

- that documents sufficiently explain the requirements and that they are accurate, listed and numbered

- that drawings required under SMM Measurement Code are ready to accompany bills to tenderers

- that any requirements for a warranty or guarantee bond are made known to tenderers at the time of invitation

ACTION **H212**	Make a final check to ascertain whether the selected firms have all completed the tendering questionnaire, and any non-collusion or other similar certificates required by the client.

NOTE

Key principles of good practice to be adopted when appointing contractors:

- *Clear procedures should be followed that ensure fair and transparent competition in a single round of tendering consisting of one or more stages.*
- *The tender process should ensure compliant, competitive tenders.*
- *Tender lists should be compiled systematically from a number of qualified contractors.*
- *Tender lists should be as short as possible.*
- *Conditions should be the same for all tenderers.*
- *Confidentiality should be respected by all parties.*
- *Sufficient time should be given for the preparation and evaluation of tenders.*
- *Sufficient information should be given for the preparation of tenders.*
- *Tenders should be assessed and accepted on quality as well as price.*
- *Practices that avoid or discourage collusion should be followed.*
- *Tender prices should not change on an unaltered scope of works.*
- *Suites of contracts and standard unamended forms of contract from recognised bodies should be used where they are available.*
- *There should be a commitment to teamwork from all parties.*

ACTION **H213**	Invite tenders for main contract works from contractors on the final tender list.	**SEE ALSO** **H/SM2**

NOTE

Follow the relevant codes of procedure for tendering to ensure fairness and reliable pricing.

- *Supply all tenderers with identical information. If queries are raised during the tendering period, deal with them promptly, and notify all other tenderers in identical terms.*

- *Do not accept late tenders.*

ACTION **H214**	Initiate action for second-stage tendering if relevant.	**SEE ALSO** **H/SM3**

NOTE

If procurement is through design and build:

- *make a final check that Employer's Requirements are complete.*

SEE ALSO
G/SM2

H

H230	Inspections/tests

ACTION H231	Arrange for tenderers to have the opportunity to inspect the site and/or existing buildings during the tender period.

ACTION H232	Arrange for tenderers to have the opportunity to inspect drawings not issued with the tender documents.

NOTE

If procurement is through design and build:

- *arrange for submission and testing of prototypes designed by contractors or specialist subcontractors, as required by tender procedure.*

- *if applicable, arrange for tenderers to submit any queries to the lead consultant for answering before tender submission. Q&A information should then be shared with all tenderers to ensure fairness and that all tenders are based on the same information.*

H260	Approvals/consents

ACTION H261	Check all necessary statutory and other consents have been obtained, and that party wall awards are in place.

NOTE

If any permissions, consents or awards are still under negotiation at this stage this could mean that alterations will be required to the tender negotiations or that start on site will be delayed.

H270	Contract and tender review

ACTION H271	Amend production information if necessary following cost checks. Establish whether changes are to be reflected in the contract documents (which will then differ from tender documents) or whether amendments are to be the subject of immediate variations under an architect's instruction issued when the contract has been entered into.
ACTION H272	Check the effects of any amendments on specialist subcontract work and arrange for adjusted tenders if necessary.
ACTION H273	Record all amendments. Identify changes clearly on revised documents. Retain and file all original issues.
ACTION H274	Manage any Q&A arising during the tendering process.
ACTION H275	Appraise, with the QS and CDMC, the tenders received and prepare a report with recommendations for the client: • Check with the cost consultant for arithmetical errors in the most acceptable tender and if any are found, use the appropriate stated procedures. • Inspect draft programmes submitted by tenderers, if required. • Arrange for the CDMC to inspect material submitted by tenderers relating to health and safety requirements, and to appraise the construction phase health and safety information submitted by the most acceptable tenderer. • Check that the tender includes information regarding the contractor's competency.
NOTE	*Deal with tender errors, or the need for a reduction, strictly in accordance with recommended procedures.*

H

| ACTION H276 | Prepare and review the tender report with the client and discuss recommendations about acceptance. |
| NOTE | *Be wary of a very low tender and explain to the client the possible risks in accepting it.* |

| ACTION H277 | If the lowest figure is greater than the amount allowed for in the cost plan, discuss with the cost consultant the most appropriate measures for reducing it, such as making alterations to the design, agree the action to be taken with the client and initiate it through negotiation or re-tendering. |

| ACTION H278 | Assist as necessary with any negotiations following consideration by the client of the most acceptable tender. |

| ACTION H279 | Continue with appraisal of tenders from specialists. Check that offers are still open for acceptance and that particulars on which they tendered are still correct. |

| ACTION H280 | Check that the CDMC has certified that the construction phase health and safety information has been developed sufficiently by the firm to be appointed as principal contractor for the construction phase to commence. |

| ACTION H281 | Notify unsuccessful tenderers of the result when the contract is signed and provide figures when appropriate. |

| NOTE | *If procurement is through design and build:* | SEE ALSO **H/SM4** |
| | *• assist the client with negotiations following the submission of the contractor's proposals and contract sum analysis, as relevant.* | |

H300 General Procedures

| ACTION H301 | Regularly check progress against the timetable for services. |

ACTION **H302**	Continue resource control procedures for job: • Check expenditure against the office job cost allocation for Stage H. • Monitor fee income against projected fee income.
ACTION **H303** NOTE	Report regularly to the client on fees and expenses incurred, and submit accounts at agreed intervals. *Check that the client settles all accounts promptly.*

H400   Stage Outputs

Check that all the agreed outputs for Stage H have been produced, which might include the following:

• main contract tenders and report with recommendations

• tenders received from specialists with appropriate forms and 'numbered documents' where appropriate

NOTE   *If procurement is through design and build:*

• *for an employer client: report for client on appraisal of contractor's proposals and contract sum analysis.*

• *for a contractor client: report for client on appraisal of tenders submitted by specialist subcontractors and suppliers; final material for incorporation into contractor's proposals and in connection with contract sum analysis.*

H

Supplementary Material

H/SM1: Selective tendering lists

The first stage in the tender process is the compilation of the tender list. Although this may not be finalised until Stage H, some preliminary enquiries can be made as soon as the overall scope, nature and approximate timescale of the work is known.

There are three steps in the selection of a contractor:

(1) qualification, in which potential contractors are assessed as to their general skills and performance in undertaking given types or a range of projects

(2) compilation of a tender list, in which the field of qualified contractors is refined to a short tender list of comparable, competent contractors who are willing and able to tender for a specific project

(3) selection of successful tenderer, in which tenders are sought from those on the tender list and assessed to identify the preferred contractor

During the period of qualification, potential contractors will normally be required to provide information about their firms and their track records. Architects will then wish to take up references and make further enquiries about those who seem suitable for inclusion in the final tender list. It is advisable to maintain a file or record of all enquiries to contractors and subcontractors and their responses.

Lists of potential contractors can be as follows.

List of contractors for larger projects

The preliminary list will be compiled from previous experience and after discussion with the client, the QS and other consultants. If a wider pool is needed, enquiries could be made of registering bodies or from www.constructionline.co.uk A questionnaire can then be sent to all those on the preliminary list to ascertain their interest in, and suitability for, the project. The questionnaire might be expected to cover:

- name and details of company
- business status of company, names of directors, etc.
- financial status, share capital, etc.
- details of quality system and accreditation
- details of insurers and liability insurance
- construction turnover and details of contracts completed recently

- particular skills and experience of relevance to the proposed project
- the personnel who would be available for the proposed project
- names of three referees
- health and safety policy and procedures
- policy on discrimination

At this initial stage the tenderers should be informed of:

- the job name and location
- nature, scope and approximate value of the works
- the proposed dates and duration of the works
- the procurement method and contract form
- any contractor responsibility for design or other particular skills or experience sought
- the selection process and criteria to be used
- details of the tender procedure to be followed, e.g. whether any particular code or principles will be followed, the numbers of tenders to be invited, the anticipated dates and period of tendering

The completed questionnaire should be signed by a director of the company. On larger projects the questionnaire might also be followed by an interview. It should then be possible to finalise the tender list. It may be wise to identify one or two contractors as reserves, in the event that, nearer the tender date, one of those on the list can no longer tender. Those on the list and reserves should be informed, and any changes to the list notified to them immediately.

List of contractors for small projects

On smaller projects contractors are generally selected by reputation or from previous experience, and after consulting the client, office records, other consultants and other sources. It would still be good practice to write to all potential contractors requesting up-to-date information about their firm and a reference, and enquiring as to their current availability and anticipated workload. This would help ensure that the tender process runs smoothly and that only suitable contractors are invited.

Approved standing list of contractors

It is often a good idea to develop a 'standing list' of approved contractors that can be drawn on at the preliminary stage of a new project. This may be particularly helpful where the office is often involved in repeat – or very similar – projects. The list could be compiled after responses to a questionnaire sent to potential tenderers. Shortlists of tenderers for future particular projects can then be drawn up as and when required.

H

The questionnaire might be expected to include the information shown above, with additional entries to indicate the type of work that the firm has experience of, and whether they would be interested in tendering for non-traditional procurement contracts.

H/SM2: Selective tendering – specialist subcontractors and suppliers

1. Identify items

During the detail design and production information stages, items where a measure of control over choice needs to be exercised should be identified. These might include for example:

- materials or suppliers named or nominated
- acceptable subcontractors restricted to listed names
- subcontractors named or nominated, as provided for by the contract

Where subcontractors or suppliers have been nominated or named under procedures laid down in the particular contract, there is usually a requirement or opportunity to use a standard design warranty in favour of the employer. However, where subcontractors or suppliers are referred to in items in the bill or specification, and are intended to be domestic appointments, the contractor will have no liability for their design input. In such cases the employer's interests might need to be protected by a warranty, should this be available. The client's consent should always be obtained in writing where subcontractors have a design input which might be regarded as having been subcontracted by the architect.

The purpose of tendering should be identified, e.g. whether it is to obtain information necessary to complete detail design, to obtain a realistic basis for a provisional sum, or to facilitate advance ordering, where desirable.

2. List suitable firms

Compile a list after discussion with other members of the design team and the contractor (if appointed). Refer to office records of previous experience and check out references if necessary.

3. Make preliminary enquiries

Consult the cost consultant and other consultants to establish a timetable for inviting tenders so as to provide necessary information for inclusion in bills/specification/schedules. Check that current information is obtained concerning the financial status of firms and that they have adequate resources. Send a preliminary invitation to tender, or to ascertain willingness for inclusion in a list of subcontractors or as a named supplier. If approximate dates and figures can be given at this stage, it should be possible to obtain a reliable response. It may be sufficient to make initial enquiries by telephone but a letter can be written if considered appropriate.

H

4. Invite tenders

Use the correct standard forms appropriate to the form of contract, and check that all relevant information is entered before sending.

Check the information to be issued with the tender form, in particular the numbered documents (e.g. drawings, schedules, bills or specification) relevant to the subcontract works. They should adequately define the work to be tendered for. A covering letter may or may not be considered necessary.

If the subcontract work is such that no particular form or set of procedures is required under the terms of the main contract, then send tender information under a suitable enclosing letter.

In the majority of cases, domestic subcontract works will be entirely a matter between the main contractor and their selected subcontractors. However, if the building contract makes provision for the architect to select subcontractors, who will nevertheless be domestic, and the contract does not require any practitioner form to be used, the architect may need to write letters of invitation to them.

There may also be situations where the architect wishes to include the name of domestic subcontractors in main contract tender documents, if the building contract does not preclude this.

5. Opening, selection and notification

Tenders should be opened as soon as possible after the date for receipt. Check that everything specified has been included. Note any omissions or added conditions and pass to the relevant consultants for comment, and to the cost consultant for cost checking.

Once a selection has been made, approve the selected tender on behalf of the employer.

Notify unsuccessful tenderers at once but do not give tender figures until a decision to proceed with the successful tenderer has been reached.

Where there is a direct subcontractor/client agreement, and only if considered desirable in the particular circumstances, issue instructions concerning advance ordering of design works, materials or fabrication. Do not do this before obtaining the client's agreement in writing.

After the appointment of the main contractor, meticulously follow the procedures set out in the main contract for instructing the acceptance of the subcontract tender. Before issuing the instruction, check that the offer is still open for acceptance, and that the particulars on which the tender was based have not changed.

H/SM3: Selective tendering: Main contract – traditional procurement

1. Decide whether single- or two-stage tendering is required

The single stage operates on the assumption that full information is available to tenderers at the time of tendering. The tender figure is then the price for which the contractor offers to carry out and complete the works shown on the drawings and described in the contract bills/specification/schedules.

Two-stage procedures allow the selection of the contractor by means of a first-stage competitive tender based on 'pricing documents' relating to preliminary design information. There will then follow negotiations when the design is completed, and bills of quantities are priced on the basis of pricing provided in the first-stage tender. This procedure is only suitable for large complex projects where there could be advantage in collaborating with the contractor during design stages.

2. Make preliminary enquiries

Send a preliminary invitation to tender to selected potential contractors. This will enable contractors to decide whether they will tender, and allow them to programme tendering staff effort. The letter of invitation should have attached to it a description of the project, relating to the form of contract it is intended to use, together with all information that might be necessary for a contractor to assess whether they are competent and interested in undertaking the project. It is essential that full details are sent in this preliminary enquiry.

3. Invite tenders

Send formal letters to tenderers informing them of the date for issuing tender documents and the closing date for submission of tenders. Documents may be dispatched by first class post or made available for collection if the number of documents is considerable.

A standard form of tender should be issued, and all tenderers clearly told that tenders will be submitted on exactly the same basis. Adequate time for tendering will be determined in relation to the size and complexity of the job.

Any particular requirements of the client concerning, for example, guarantee bonds or a certificate of non-collusion should be clearly stated in the formal invitation.

4. Opening, selection and notification

Tenders should be opened as soon as possible after the date for receipt, and strictly in accordance with the procedures agreed with the client. Qualified

H

tenders should be rejected if it is considered that the qualification affords an unfair advantage, or the tenderer should be given an opportunity to withdraw the qualification.

The priced bills of quantities should be submitted at the same time as the tenders but in separate sealed envelopes clearly marked with the tenderers' names. Bills from unsuccessful tenderers should be returned unopened.

Tenders under consideration should be referred to the CDMC to check adequacy of allocated resources in respect of health and safety requirements.

Examination of the priced bills of the lowest tenderer should be undertaken immediately by the cost consultant, who should report on arithmetical errors.

Unsuccessful tenderers should be informed as quickly as possible, and once the contract has been let, every tenderer should be sent a list of firms who tendered (in alphabetical order) and a list of tender prices (in ascending order). It should not be possible to cross-reference the lists.

H/SM4: Selective tendering: Main contract – design and build procurement

1. Make preliminary enquiries

Send a preliminary invitation to tender to selected potential contractors. This will enable contractors to decide whether they will tender, and allow them to programme tendering staff effort. The letter of invitation should have attached to it a description of the project, relating to the form of contract it is intended to use, together with all information that might be necessary for the contractor to assess whether it is competent and interested in undertaking the project. It is essential that full details are sent in this preliminary enquiry. In particular, for design and build, the letter of invitation should clearly state whether this is a single-stage or a two-stage process, and the extent to which the contractor will be expected to design the works and carry professional indemnity insurance.

The letter should have attached to it information relating to planning requirements, e.g. whether the project is within a conservation area, etc.

Tenderers will also need to know the basis for awarding the contract, e.g. on price alone, and if not, the extent to which other considerations will be taken into account, such as design quality, maintenance or running costs.

2. Arrange interviews

It is particularly important to arrange for interviews in the context of design and build. Matters to be raised might include:

- construction forms and methods favoured
- time considered appropriate for tendering and mobilisation
- design liability and insurance arrangements
- professional and technical support available to the contractor
- design and construction programme envisaged by the contractor

The interviewing panel should include the client, the CDMC and appropriate professional advisers.

3. Invite tenders

Send formal letters to selected tenderers either enclosing the tender documents in duplicate or informing them of the date for collection. The extent of these documents will depend on whether the tendering is single or two stage, but should include everything that is intended to form part of the final agreement (see G/SM2 for a checklist of what might be included in Employer's Requirements).

H

A standard form of tender should be issued. Adequate time for tendering will depend on the size and complexity of the project, and whether this is a single- or two-stage submission.

4. Opening, selection and notification

Tenders should be opened as soon as possible after the date for receipt and strictly in accordance with the procedures agreed with the client.

With a single-stage procedure where price is stated to be the sole criterion, supporting design proposals and pricing documents should be submitted at the same time but under separate cover.

With a two-stage procedure the tender will also include an undertaking to enter into second-stage negotiations on the basis of the first-stage tender sum.

The examination of the contractor's proposals and pricing documents will be undertaken by the employer, the CDMC and other professional advisers, to establish that the proposals are consistent with the Employer's Requirements.

Unsuccessful tenderers should be informed as quickly as possible, and all documents received should be treated as confidential, and returned.

H/SM5: Selective tendering: Main contract – management procurement

1. Make preliminary enquiries

Send a preliminary invitation to tender to selected potential contractors. This will enable contractors to decide whether they will tender, and allow them to programme tendering staff effort. The letter of invitation should have attached to it a description of the project, the form of contract it is intended to use, the anticipated duration of the project pre-construction and construction, together with all information that might be necessary for the contractor to assess whether it is competent and interested in undertaking the project. It is essential that full details are sent in this preliminary enquiry.

With management contracting, the emphasis will be on ascertaining the nature and extent of the contractor's management skills and experience.

2. Arrange preliminary interviews

Because of the large or complex management nature of projects usually procured by this method, it might be necessary also to hold preliminary interviews at this stage. This will enable the employer to gain a better understanding of the philosophy and management structure offered by some of the potential firms, to an extent not possible solely through written enquiries.

3. Invite tenders

Send formal letters to selected tenderers. Tender documents should contain:

- clear conditions for the submission, so that all tenderers provide the same amount of information
- proposed timescales pre-construction and construction
- a clear indication of the assessment and interview procedures that will form part of the overall assessment

Criteria to be satisfied will normally include:

- management service offered
- key personnel for the project
- financial: in respect of both fees and ability to manage costs
- conditions of engagement
- programmes
- method statements

H

4. Opening, selection and notification

Tenders should be opened as soon as possible after the date for receipt, and strictly in accordance with the procedure agreed with the client.

A detailed evaluation of each submission should be prepared. When the written submissions have undergone preliminary evaluation they can be assessed by the employer. It will then be necessary to interview each tenderer. This will enable them to explain their proposals in detail, and clarify any points in the submission which need comment, and allow the employer to meet the key personnel that the tenderer proposes using. Further interviews may be necessary before a decision is reached.

Unsuccessful tenderers should be informed as soon as possible.

Mobilisation

STAGE DESCRIPTION

As defined in *RIBA Outline Plan of Work 2007*:

■ Letting the building contract, appointing the contractor

■ Issuing of information to the contractor

■ Arranging site handover to the contractor

CONTENTS

J

Stage Description

In the strict sense of the term, mobilisation is likely to be mainly the responsibility of the appointed contractor. However, an architect acting as the lead consultant can do much at this stage to see that the contract is properly set up from the outset.

Contract documents have to be prepared, and the agreement should be signed before work on site commences. There will need to be an exchange of information between architect and contractor, and confirmed agreement on procedures to be followed.

The client will enter into the building contract as the employer, and the site given into the possession of the contractor so that work may proceed as programmed. The employer, contractor and relevant consultants will need to be advised on their respective responsibilities under the contract.

The contractor must have reasonable time to mobilise resources. Client and contractor insurances for the construction period will need to be put in place and checked. Site inspectorate will need to be appointed and briefed. Arrangements should be made for the formal initial project team meeting, sometimes also referred to as the pre-start or pre-contract meeting.

This stage is the point of novation or 'consultant switch' under design and build procurement.

J

Key Obligations

(from RIBA Agreements 2007: Standard Agreements (S-Con-07): Schedule of Design Services (SS-DS-07))

Provide construction information as required for and by the building contract.

J100	**Preliminary Issues**

J110	**Information required**

Check that all information necessary during Stage J is available, which might include the following:

- form of contract, with all necessary entries and supplements, ready for completion by the parties

- contract documents, including drawings and bills of quantities/specification/schedules of work, incorporating any necessary adjustments, ready for issue

- completed tender documents from the successful tenderer

- written records of any post-tender changes to the contracted project

- administration forms published for use in contract administration, suitable for the particular contract to be used

- contractor's preliminary programme and required method statements

J120	**Appointment**

ACTION J121

Establish scope, content and context for Stage J activities.

NOTE

Put it into context, particularly if previous stages were undertaken by others. If possible establish whether material produced now is likely to be acted upon by others taking over subsequent stages.

If the appointment includes Stage L2, the architect must discuss with the contractor the initial occupation provisions specified in the building contract.

If the appointment includes Stage L3, the architect must discuss with the contractor the specified review provisions.

J

ACTION J122	If coming new to the project at this stage in the Plan of Work:

- Ascertain that Pre-Agreement and earlier stage checks have been carried out.

- Agree fees and timetable with the client.

NOTE *Allow for familiarisation and reviewing of all usable material when agreeing fees and timetable with the client.*

- Confirm the role of the architect in relation to the rest of the consultant team.

- Ensure that you have the necessary competency and resource to undertake the work and address the H&S issues likely to be involved in it.

- Request a copy of the project-specific, pre-construction health and safety information and review it.

- Re-advise the client in writing of their responsibilities under the CDM Regulations and ensure that a CDMC has been appointed.

NOTE *Where a project is notifiable, the regulations require that the client appoints a CDMC as soon as is practicable after initial design work or other preparation for construction work has begun. This would generally be at Stage C.*

- Ensure that you have adequate professional indemnity insurance cover.

ACTION J123	Check that the client's instruction to proceed has been given and confirmed in writing.

ACTION J124	Check that the client has settled all accounts submitted to date.

ACTION J125	Check appointing documents with respect to services and fees:

- If the services, cost or time targets are different from the agreement with the client, agree a formal variation by letter or deed as appropriate.

- If the extent of professional services for Stage J is not yet settled, agree with the client and confirm in writing.

- If the methods and levels of charging for Stage J are not yet settled, agree with the client and confirm in writing.

| ACTION J126 | Assess office resources needed for Stage J and ensure that they are available and adequate. |

| ACTION J127 | Confirm contract administration and site inspection services and frequency and procedures for site visits for Stage K. |

J130 Client

| ACTION J131 | If a clerk of works is to be appointed, check whether the client has confirmed the appointment. |

| ACTION J132 | Remind the client that any insurances for which they have accepted responsibility should have been taken out. Policies should be kept available for inspection by the contractor at all reasonable times. | SEE ALSO **J/SM4** |

| ACTION J133 | Discuss with the client the main contractor's master programme. Draw to the client's attention significant dates by which any further decisions or information will be needed, and by which any persons directly employed are programmed to start and finish. |

| ACTION J134 | Confirm to the client the responsibilities and obligations under the contract as employer. Confirm the architect's role and duties as agent and contract administrator. |

| ACTION J135 | Remind the client of the obligation to honour certificates of payment in full and within the period stated in the contract. |
| NOTE | *Explain the notices' provisions in detail. If any deduction is intended from amounts certified, it will be essential to issue notices as required by the contract.* |

| ACTION J136 | Remind the client that empowered instructions to the contractor can only be issued by way of an architect's instruction. |

| ACTION J137 | If procurement is through design and build:

For an employer client: check whether the client has confirmed the appointment of an employer's agent. The authority of this person should be clearly stated in writing, and the contractor should be informed. |

J

J150	**Consultant team**

ACTION **J151**	Check the scope of professional services agreed with the client for continued presence of the consultant team members as members of the project team.

ACTION **J152**	Agree the scope and timetable for any amendments needed to contract documents as a result of post-tender negotiations.

ACTION **J153**	Agree with the cost consultant a timetable for the preparation of a bill of reductions or similar document setting out agreed adjustments to the tender figure, if relevant.

ACTION **J154**	Brief the site inspectorate.	SEE ALSO **J/SM2**
NOTE	*Site inspectorate who are under the direction of the architect should be thoroughly briefed. Give the clerk of works clear instructions on procedures and reporting.*	

ACTION **J155**	Confirm dates for construction phase with the client and CDMC.

J200	**Stage Activities**

J260	**Approvals/consents**

ACTION **J261**	Check that any necessary approvals and consents have been obtained and are on file. If any are still outstanding, explain to the client the consequences of starting on site prematurely.

ACTION **J262**	Check that all notices granting planning permission and approval under Building Regulations are to hand. Check that statutory approvals are still valid within time limits.

| ACTION J263 | Check that the Health and Safety Executive has been given particulars required by law under the CDM Regulations. |

| ACTION J264 | Check with the client that all necessary party wall awards are in place. |

J370 Contract

| ACTION J271 | Review post-tender situation. In the event of an omission or a substitution necessitating revisions to detail design, take appropriate action if authorised by the client. Alert the client to any additional costs, fees or alterations to programme. |
| NOTE | *Post-tender cost reduction exercises usually mean additional work. Allow time for this.* |

ACTION J272	Confirm dates for commencement and completion.
	Clarify any queries from the contractor.
	Establish and inspect contractor's programmes and confirm information schedules.

| ACTION J273 | Call for all the contractor's insurance policies. Pass on to the employer for checking by his brokers or insurance advisers. | SEE ALSO J/SM4 |
| NOTE | Check original documents carefully for cover and renewal dates. Do not accept assurances. | |

| ACTION J274 | Check bonds and warranties required from the contractor. |
| NOTE | *These should be obtained before the contract is signed – it may be impossible to obtain them later.* |

| ACTION J275 | Check that the CDMC has expressed satisfaction with the contractor's construction phase Health and Safety Plan, and that this is confirmed in writing. |

J

ACTION **J276**	Prepare contract documents for signature. Send by registered/ recorded post or deliver by hand. It is customary to send these first to the contractor and then to the employer.	SEE ALSO **G/SM1** **J/SM1**
NOTE	*When preparing contract documents for signature or completion as a deed, check meticulously that entries are correct, and relate to tender documents. If more than one copy, check that they are identical.*	
ACTION **J277**	Collate approved specialist tender documents for issue to the contractor.	
ACTION **J278**	Check that parties have properly signed contract documents and any agreed alterations are initialled.	
ACTION **J279**	Check that all unsuccessful tenderers have been properly notified.	
ACTION **J280**	Check that additional copies of drawings and other documents are handed to the main contractor as required by the contract. Issue identical set to the clerk of works. If an Information Release Schedule does not form part of the contract, agree with the contractor a schedule for further necessary information.	
ACTION **J281**	Carefully inspect the contractor's preliminary programme, particularly if it indicates dates by which critical information is required. Comment as appropriate but do not approve it.	
ACTION **J282**	Check that the contractor has prepared a Health and Safety Plan which is acceptable to the CDMC.	
NOTE	*Under no circumstances can work start on site without a Health and Safety Plan in place which conforms with the CDM Regulations.*	
ACTION **J283**	Check quality management proposals and procedures with the contractor.	
ACTION **J284**	Check proposed site planning and accommodation with the contractor.	

ACTION **J285**	Hold an initial project team meeting with the employer, main contractor, consultants, cost consultant and clerk of works. Chair the initial project meeting, if appropriate, and issue minutes.	SEE ALSO **J/SM3**
NOTE	*When chairing the initial project team meeting, be fair, firm and pleasant. This is an opportunity to make relevant introductions and establish clear procedures.*	

| ACTION **J286** | Arrange for the handover of site and/or existing buildings, allowing the contractor exclusive possession or to the extent previously agreed. |

J290 Cost planning

| ACTION **J291** | Check with the quantity surveyor, if appointed, the contractor's schedule of rates and the contract sum analysis where relevant. |

J300 General Procedures

| ACTION **J301** | Regularly check progress against the timetable for services. |

| ACTION **J302** | Continue resource control procedures for job (usually monthly):
• Check expenditure against the office job cost allocation for Stage J.
• Monitor fee income against projected fee income. |

ACTION **J303**	Report regularly to the client on fees and expenses incurred, and submit accounts at agreed intervals (usually monthly).
NOTE	*Check that the client settles all accounts promptly.*

ACTION J304	Set up procedures for ensuring that drawings and other information are prepared and provided to the contractor as required, or as set out in the contract.
ACTION J305	Set up accounts procedures for invoicing the appointed main contractor monthly for the cost of copies of drawings and documents additional to those stated in the contract, whether these involve prints or software.
ACTION J306	Compile a directory of all involved at construction stages.
ACTION J307	Check stationery stocks for correct and current contract administration forms.

J400   Stage Outputs

Check that all the agreed outputs for Stage J have been produced, which might include the following:

- bill of reductions or similar document setting out agreed adjustments to the tender figure, if relevant, to arrive at an acceptable contract figure

- contract documents duly signed and initialled as appropriate by employer and contractor as parties to the contract

- requisite sets of drawings, schedules and other documents for issue to the main contractor

- approved tenders and numbered documents in respect of specialist subcontractors for issue to main contractor

- construction phase Health and Safety Plan and HSE notification by main contractor

- requisite forms and documents for issue to the clerk of works if appropriate

Supplementary Material

J/SM1: Dealing with contract documents

Notifying all tenderers

A letter should be sent to the selected tenderer confirming the decision to accept the tender. This may be subject to agreed modifications to the contracted works, usually to fit within the cost plan. This letter might state that a contract will not exist until the documents have been prepared and signed by the parties. If this is so, it is important to make sure that the signing of the contract takes place before the date agreed for possession, to avoid possible allegations of frustration.

Once the tender has been accepted, a list of compliant tender prices and tenderers should be sent to all tenderers within a reasonable period of time.

As a general rule the formalities of the contract agreement should always be completed before work starts on site. While the use of a letter of intent is to be avoided where possible, in certain circumstances it may be necessary or desirable to allow design, procurement and possibly even construction to be commenced prior to finalisation and resolution of all contractual matters between parties. The City of London Law Society has produced a standard letter of intent and guidance notes which can be found at www.citysolicitors.org.uk. The letter seeks to provide a standard form document that covers typical issues arising but each situation should be reviewed on its own terms and legal advice sought as necessary.

Under no circumstances should construction work be started before the contractor has prepared a Health and Safety Plan which complies with the CDM Regulations.

Completing the contract documents

Both parties should enter into a contract on the basis of a complete set of documents, each of which has been completed as necessary (see G/SM1 for a list of contract documents).

The agreement between the employer and the contractor should be dated and should reflect the correct titles and addresses of the parties. Normally the addresses will be those to which notices, instructions, certificates, etc. are to be sent. If either party wishes to have all contractual communications sent to a different address, this should be recorded in the contract documents.

J

Signing the contract

The form of building contract containing the Articles of Agreement is normally sent first to the contractor, accompanied by the drawings listed in the Recitals and the other contract documents as appropriate. Pencil in a cross to indicate where the contractor is to sign (usually in the lower set of spaces). Documents returned by the contractor should be examined carefully to see that they have been completed properly, as requested in the covering letter.

The documents should then be passed to the employer with a covering letter asking the employer to date the Articles. Documents returned from the employer should be examined carefully to see that they have been completed properly.

Signing confirmed

Instead of signing separately, the parties may agree to meet at some convenient place and complete the execution of the contract in each other's presence.

If the contract is to be executed as a simple contract, only the signatures of both parties are necessary. The signatures of witnesses – desirable, although not a legal necessity – confirm the existence of the agreement.

If the contract is to be executed as a deed, then appropriate wording should be used for the attestation clause. Special wording may be required depending on the memorandum or standing orders of an authority or corporate body.

The manner of execution of the main contract does not necessarily mean that subcontracts or collateral agreements have to be similarly executed. However, thought should be given to this matter so as to avoid confusion and unnecessary complications and costs.

It is sometimes stated in the contract conditions who is to have custody of the original contract documents – usually the employer. The documents should be kept in a secure fireproof place. Copies of the contract documents should be suitably endorsed, for example, 'This is a certified copy of the Agreement dated . . . between . . . and . . .' and signed by the architect. A set is given to the contractor and the architect would be wise to keep another complete set safe in the office.

Note that contracts executed under Scottish law will have different wording for the attestation.

J/SM2: Site inspectorate appointment and briefing

On large works, full-time resident consultants (e.g. architects, engineers) or the clerk of works might be needed to monitor conformity of materials, construction and quality, and also to liaise on the many activities upon which the full standards of the building's performance will depend.

On most large contracts a clerk of works is a full-time and valuable presence. The clerk of works must appreciate the extent of their powers and duties which are generally to observe, inspect, check and report. With JCT contracts, the clerk of works operates under the direction of the architect/contract administrator and must be thoroughly conversant with the form of contract.

The clerk of works' manual is a useful source of information. It sets out standard terms of appointment, defines duties and responsibilities, lists the documents which the clerk of works should maintain and offers a range of forms which might assist both the clerk of works and the architect.

Clerk of works reporting

A site diary is essential for recording day-to-day events. There is also a need to provide the architect with periodic reports to record progress on site, usually on a weekly basis. Printed forms will be provided for the clerk of works to complete and sign. The Institute of Clerks of Works publishes a Project Report form which will be suitable for most situations, see Fig. J1.

J

J/SM3: Pre-contract meeting

This meeting, sometimes referred to as the pre-start meeting, is crucial.

The site inspectorate may have already been briefed at separate meetings, or the briefing could form part of the initial project team meeting. At the meeting, all personnel will be introduced, and lines of communication can be unequivocally identified and defined. This is the first opportunity for all the project team to meet and for effective working arrangements to be established.

It is essential for the person identified as the contract administrator to know the full range of contractual requirements of the project, and to be alert to potentially difficult areas. As chairman of the meeting, this person must establish mutual confidence and see that different viewpoints are aired and accommodated before the project gets under way.

The business of the meeting is likely to cover a wide range of topics and it is important to start with a clear agenda and stick to it. For a specimen agenda, see Fig. J1.

Agenda items at pre-contract meeting

Introductions

- Introduce the representatives who will regularly attend progress meetings and clarify their roles and responsibilities. The client, contractor and consultants may wish to introduce themselves.
- Briefly describe the project and its priorities and objectives, and any separate contract which may be relevant (preliminary, client's own contractors, etc.).
- Indicate any specialists appointed by the client, e.g. for quality control, commissioning, for this contract.

Contract

- Describe the present position with regard to preparation and signature of documents.
- Hand over any outstanding production information, including nomination instructions, variation instructions. Review situation for issuing other important information.
- Request that insurance documents be available for inspection immediately; remind the contractor to check specialist subcontractors' indemnities. Check whether further instructions are needed for special cover.
- Confirm the existence, status and use of the Information Release Schedule, if used. Establish procedure for agreeing adjustments to the Schedule should they be necessary.

- Confirm contractor's status and role as competent constructor under the CDM Regulations.

Contractor's matters

- Check that the contractor's master programme is in the form required and that it satisfactorily accommodates the specialist subcontractors. It must:

  - contain adequate separate work elements to measure their progress and integration with services installations
  - allocate specific dates for specialist subcontract works, including supply of information, site operations, testing and commissioning
  - accommodate public utilities, etc.

- Agree a procedure for the contractor to inform the architect of information required in addition to any shown on the Information Release Schedule. This is likely to involve a contractor's schedule of information required, which must relate to its works programme and must be kept up to date and regularly reviewed. It should include information, data, drawings, etc. to be supplied by the contractor/specialist subcontractors to the architect/consultants.
- Review in detail the particular provisions in the contract concerning site access, organisation, facilities, restrictions, services, etc. to ensure that no queries remain outstanding.
- Quality control is the contractor's responsibility. Remind the contractor of the contractual duties to supervise, of your duties to inspect, and the clerk of works'/site inspectorate's duties in connection with the works. Clarify what standards, quality of work and management are required during the execution of the works.
- Numerous other matters may need special coverage, e.g.

  - Check whether immediate action may be needed by the contractor over specialist subcontractors and suppliers.
  - Emphasise that drawings, data, etc. received from the contractor or specialist subcontractors will be inspected by the architect/consultants (not approved), and will remain the responsibility of the originator.
  - Review outstanding requirements for information to or from the contractor in connection with specialist works.
  - Clarify that the contractor is responsible for coordinating the performance of specialist works and for their workmanship and materials, for providing specialists with working facilities and for coordinating site dimensions and tolerances.

- The contractor must also provide for competent testing and commissioning of services as set out in the contract documents, and should be reminded that the time allocated for commissioning is not a contingency period for the main contract works.

J

- The contractor must obtain the architect's written consent before subletting any work.

Clerk of works' matters

- Clarify that architect's inspections are periodic visits to meet the contractor's supervisory staff, plus spot visits.
- Explain the supportive nature of the clerk of works' role, and the need for cooperation to enable them to carry out their duties.
- Remind the contractor that the clerk of works must be provided with adequate facilities and access, together with information about site staff, equipment and operations, for the clerk of works' weekly reports to the architect.
- Confirm procedures for checking quality control, e.g. through:

  - certificates, vouchers, etc. as required
  - sample material to be submitted
  - samples of workmanship to be submitted prior to work commencing
  - test procedures set out in the bills of quantities
  - adequate protection and storage
  - visits to suppliers'/manufacturers' works

Consultants' matters

- Emphasise that consultants will liaise with specialist subcontractors only through the contractor. Instructions are to be issued only by the architect. The contractor is responsible for managing and coordinating specialist subcontractors.
- Establish working arrangements for specialists' drawings and data for evaluation (especially services) to suitable timetables. Aim to agree procedures which will speed up the process; this sector of work frequently causes serious delay or disruption.

Communications and procedures

- The supply and flow of information will depend upon programmes being established at the start and will proceed smoothly if:

  - there is regular monitoring of the information schedules
  - requests for further information are made specifically in writing, not by telephone
  - the architect responds quickly to queries
  - technical queries are raised with the clerk of works (if appointed) in the first instance
  - policy queries are directed to the architect
  - discrepancies are referred to the architect for resolution, not the clerk of works or contractor

- On receiving instructions, check for discrepancies with existing documents; check that documents being used are current.
- Information to or from specialist subcontractors or suppliers must be via the contractor.
- All information issued by the architect is to be via the appropriate forms, certificates, notifications, etc. The contractor should be encouraged to use standard formats and classifications.
- All forms must show the distribution intended; agree numbers of copies of drawings and instructions required by all recipients.
- Clarify that no instructions from the client or consultants can be accepted by the contractor or any subcontractor; only empowered written instructions by the architect are valid, and all verbal instructions must be confirmed in writing. Explain the relevant procedures under the contract. The contractor should promptly notify the architect of any written confirmations outstanding.
- Procedures for notices, applications or claims of any kind are to be strictly in accordance with the terms of the contract; all such events should be raised immediately the relevant conditions occur or become evident.

Meetings

- Always issue an agenda beforehand for all architect's meetings, and circulate minutes promptly. Agree with the contractor and consultants that:

  - minutes are to be taken as directions for action only where specifically stated and agreed
  - any dissent is to be notified within seven days
  - all persons attending will have authority to act

- Agree copies and distribution required.

See also Stage K for a summary of the various types of meeting for project administration, and the specimen agenda for the progress meetings, Fig. K2. See Stage K for advice about site inspections.

J

J/SM4: Insurances check

Insurance in the context of building construction is a highly specialised area but one of great importance for the contract administrator. Certain insurance obligations arise from legislation but the building contract will usually contain specific requirements concerning insurance cover against injury or damage caused during the works.

These requirements will have been discussed with the client, and the implications fully explained, prior to tender stage. The cost of insurance premiums will have been taken into account by the tenderers. Responsibility for the required cover, whether taken out by the contractor or the employer, will have been established.

Whereas the checking of policy wording is a matter for insurance experts advising either the contractor or the employer as relevant, it is for the contract administrator to check that the obligations to take out cover have been complied with.

An insurances check is necessary before any work on site is commenced. Although most contractors carry an annual policy, endorsements and some cover can take time to arrange. It may be that in some circumstances it proves impossible to obtain the cover stated, in which case it will be for the parties to the contract to decide the arrangements to apply.

Specialist subcontractors are sometimes mainly responsible for damage which occurs and such an eventuality must be properly covered. The employer pays the cost of insurance in the end and it is important to avoid the risk of double insurance. Cover must be adequate and any figures entered in the building contract should be realistic after taking expert advice on the particular circumstances. The mere repetition of some previously quoted sum is a recipe for disaster.

At mobilisation stage it is vital to ensure that the required insurances are in place before work commences.

Figures

Figure J1: Specimen agenda for pre-contract meeting

Job no: Job title:

Agenda for pre-contract meeting

1 Introductions

- Appointments, personnel
- Roles and responsibilities
- Project description

2 Contract

- Priorities
- Handover of production information
- Commencement and completion dates
- Insurances
- Bonds (if applicable)
- Standards and quality

3 Contractor's matters

- Possession
- Programme
- Health and Safety file and plan
- Site organisations, facilities and planning
- Security and protection
- Site restrictions
- Contractor's quality control policy and procedures
- Sub-contractors and suppliers
- Statutory undertakers
- Overhead and underground services
- Temporary services
- Signboards

4 Clerk of works' matters

- Roles and duties
- Facilities
- Liaison
- Dayworks

5 Consultants' matters

- Architectural
- Structural
- Mechanical
- Electrical
- Others

6 Quantity surveyor's matters

- Adjustments to tender figures
- Valuation procedures
- Remeasurement
- VAT

7 Communications and procedures

- Information requirements
- Distribution of information
- Valid instructions
- Lines of communications
- Dealing with queries
- Building Control notices
- Notices to adjoining owners/ occupiers

8 Meetings

- Pattern and proceedings
- Status of minutes
- Distribution of minutes

J

Construction to Practical Completion

STAGE DESCRIPTION

As defined in *RIBA Outline Plan of Work 2007*:

■ Administration of building contract to practical completion
■ Provision to the contractor of further information as and when reasonably required
■ Review of information provided by contractors and specialists

CONTENTS

CONTINUES

K

262

CONTENTS (CONTINUED)

Stage Description

The architect may be nominated as the contract administrator. The terms of the building contract bind only the parties themselves, i.e. the employer and the contractor; they do not place contractual obligations on the architect. Nevertheless, should the architect as contract administrator fail in the procedural duties set out, for example not issuing a certificate as required, this could constitute a breach of contract on the part of the employer against whom the contractor may be able to claim losses. It is therefore important that the architect's contract for professional services reflects accurately their role under the construction contract.

With traditional procurement, the contractor normally undertakes to carry out and complete the works in accordance with the contract, to proceed regularly and diligently, to complete by the agreed completion date and to comply with instructions empowered by the contract.

The client or employer normally undertakes to give the contractor possession in order to carry out the work, ensure that all necessary information is made available to the contractor, appoint a contract administrator and pay all amounts properly certified or due under the contract.

With traditional procurement, the role of the contract administrator will vary considerably depending on the particular form used but the administrator would normally issue necessary information to the contractor, issue instructions empowered or required by the contract, issue certificates as required by the contract, and would be required to act in a fair and reasonable manner where impartial judgement is required by the contract.

Design and build procurement

There is normally no role for an impartial contract administrator with design and build procurement. The architect will therefore have no direct involvement in contract administration. Where acting for an employer client, consultancy advice might be needed, or an architect might be appointed as the employer's agent. Where acting for a contractor client, any involvement will not go beyond giving consultancy advice. The authority of the employer's agent comes from the employer, not the construction contract, and the employer's agent has no duties under the construction contract.

Management procurement

With management procurement there is usually the need for an independent contract administrator whose duties will normally include the issue of necessary

K

information and instructions, and the issue of certificates. The obligations of the contractor will differ from those under traditional procurement and will be fully described in the contract.

Key Obligations

(from RIBA Agreements 2007: Standard Agreements (S-Con-07): Schedule of Design Services (SS-DS-07))

Make visits to construction works as designer.

Provide further information reasonably required for construction.

Review design information from contractors or specialists.

Provide drawings showing the building and main lines of drainage and other information, where applicable, for the Health and Safety File (CDM 2007) and the building log book (Building Regulations Approved Document L2).

Review compliance with statutory and contract requirements.

Give general advice on operation and maintenance of the building.

Prepare and submit to client a Stage K report.

K100   Preliminary Issues

K110   Information required

Check that all information necessary during Stage K is available, which might include the following:

- coordinated production information: drawings, drawn schedules, priced bills of quantities/specification/schedules of work

- contractor's rates or contract sum analysis if appropriate, and/or priced bills of quantities/specification/schedules of work

- specialists' tenders and 'numbered documents' ready for nomination instruction to be issued

- contractor's Master Programme

- copies of the construction phase Health and Safety Plan developed by the contractor and certified by the CDMC

- copies of method statements prepared by the contractor as required in the contract conditions

- information release schedule, or

- schedule agreed with contractor indicating what further information is needed from the architect and by when, or

- verification by the contractor, if applicable, that all necessary information has been supplied, and accepting that any further drawings will be their own responsibility

- sets of administration forms appropriate for the form of contract being used

K

K120 Appointment

ACTION **K121**	Establish scope, content and context for Stage K activities.

Put it into context, particularly if previous stages were undertaken by others. If possible establish whether material produced now is likely to be acted upon by others taking over subsequent Stages.

If the appointment includes Stage L2, the architect must: review design information from contractors or specialists for compliance with occupation and facilities management strategies; review and monitor contractor's building readiness programme; prepare building users' guide and contribute to periodic reports.

If the appointment includes Stage L3, the architect must identify any changes to targets, and their causes, and contribute to periodic reports.

ACTION **K122**	If coming new to the project at this stage in the Plan of Work:

- Ascertain that the relevant Pre-Agreement and earlier Stage checks have been carried out.

- Confirm scope and frequency of site meetings, visits and issuing of interim certificates.

Allow for familiarisation and reviewing of all usable material when agreeing fees and timetable with the client.

- Confirm the role of the architect in relation to the rest of the consultant team.

- Ensure that you have the necessary competency and resource to undertake the work and address the H&S issues likely to be involved in it.

- Request a copy of the project-specific, pre-construction health and safety information and review it.

- Advise the client of their responsibilities under the CDM Regulations and ensure that a CDMC has been appointed.

Where a project is notifiable, the regulations require that the client appoints a CDMC as soon as is practicable after initial design work or other preparation for construction work has begun. This would generally be at Stage C.

- Ensure that you have adequate professional indemnity insurance cover.

ACTION **K123**	Check the client's written instruction to proceed.

ACTION **K124**	Check that the client has settled all accounts submitted to date.

ACTION **K125**	Check appointing documents with respect to services and fees. • If the services, cost or time targets are different from the agreement with the client, agree a formal variation by letter or deed, as appropriate. • If the extent of professional services for Stage K is not yet settled, agree with the client and confirm in writing. **NOTE** *Remember that the agreed services must reflect the role of architect under the form of building contract selected. Inform the client in advance if more frequent visits are required than those allowed for in the agreement and which would incur additional expenditure.*

ACTION **K126**	Assess office resources needed for Stage K and ensure that they are available and adequate.

K130	**Client**

ACTION **K131**	Check with the client that the contract documents have been completed and signed as a simple contract or a deed as applicable.

ACTION **K132**	Check that the site or existing buildings have been given into the possession of the appointed contractor for the duration of the works.

ACTION **K133**	Remind the client of relevant statutory obligations under the CDM Regulations relating to the role of the CDMC and the competence of the principal contractor and other contractors' performance in health and safety matters.

ACTION **K134**	Advise the client of the employer's obligations under the building contract and of the role and duties of the architect in administering the building contract.

K

ACTION K135	Remind the client that all instructions to the main contractor must be channelled through the architect.
ACTION K136	Remind the client of the obligation to honour monetary certificates within the periods stated in the contract and of the procedure, should any deduction be anticipated, for example in respect of liquidated damages.
ACTION K137	Explain to the client the implications of practical completion. Advise the client, should partial possession be desired, about the contractual implications and procedures.
ACTION K138	Discuss with the client the need to appoint maintenance staff in time to attend the commissioning of the project, and to enter into maintenance agreements if relevant.
ACTION K139	Discuss with the client the requirements for 'as built' information and maintenance manuals.
ACTION K140	Remind the client of the requirement for a Health and Safety File to be deposited in a safe place at the completion of the project.

K150 Consultant team

ACTION K151	Convene and chair site progress meetings or attend progress meetings chaired by the contractor.	SEE ALSO K/SM2
NOTE	*Methodically keep accurate minutes of meetings, and record discussions, progress statements and decisions. In assessing subsequent claims or allegations, these records may prove invaluable and more than justify the effort needed to maintain them.*	
ACTION K152	Confirm that all instructions concerning specialist subcontractors or suppliers are to be channelled through the architect. If acceptable, they will be included under an architect's instruction issued to the main contractor.	

ACTION K153	Confirm that consultants are to supply relevant information for the preparation of operating instructions, maintenance manuals, record drawings of installation, etc.
ACTION K154	Check the designers' cooperation with the CDMC.
ACTION K155	Confirm that consultants are to pass relevant information to the CDMC for inclusion in the Health and Safety File.
ACTION K156	Confirm that consultants are to carry out detailed inspection of specialist work and report to the architect. If authorised, they should also attend commissioning, testing and witnessing, and report.
ACTION K157	Confirm with the client and QS the procedures for valuation and certification.
ACTION K158	Confirm arrangements for reporting regularly to the client, and for providing regular financial reports.

K200   Stage Activities

K230   Inspections/tests

ACTION K231	Confirm programme and procedures for the architect's site visits.	SEE ALSO K/SM3
ACTION K232	Brief site inspection staff, including the clerk of works if appointed, about their duties and the procedures to be followed.	

NOTE	*Visit the site as provided for in the agreement with the client, whether for periodic checks, predictive checks or spot checks, to observe and comment on the contractor's site supervision and examples of work.*

K

| ACTION K233 | Prepare an inspection plan which identifies when visits should be made, and when checks can be made on tests which the contractor is obliged to make under the contract, including visits by building control. | |

ACTION K234	Keep methodical records of all site visits and results of all tests witnessed or reported.	SEE ALSO **Fig. K3**
NOTE	*Allow adequate time on site to carry out checks properly. Make careful notes and compile a systematic record of visits. It helps to prepare checklists relating to the stage of the work.*	
	Check that work is being executed generally in accordance with the provisions of the building contract, in a proper and workmanlike manner and in accordance with the Health and Safety Plan.	

| ACTION K235 | Inspect the contractor's progress measured against the master programme, and generally inspect goods and materials delivered to the site. | |

| ACTION K236 | Check the contractor's quality management performance measured against the plan submitted in the contractor's method statement. | |

K270   Contract

| ACTION K271 | Provide the contractor with copies of contract documents as required under the contract. | |

ACTION K272	Meet the contractor on site to note setting out, including boundaries, fencing and hoardings, site huts, amenities and welfare arrangements, protective measures, spoil heaps, etc. to establish compliance with contractor's method statements and contract requirements.	
NOTE	*Administer the contract in accordance with the procedural rules and the conditions, acting fairly and impartially between the parties.*	
	It is essential to acquire a good knowledge and understanding of all the contract documents. Keep a copy to hand at all times.	

NOTE *Issue architect's instructions, discretionary or obligatory, as empowered under the contract, and in accordance with the contract provisions:*

- *All instructions to the contractor should be in writing. It is good practice to issue them on an architect's instruction form (not via correspondence or site meeting minutes).*

- *Only empowered instructions should be issued. Keep the wording concise and unambiguous.*

- *Confirm oral instructions as soon as necessary to avoid difficulties and to ensure that cost appraisals are realistic.*

ACTION
K273 Provide information as set out on the information release schedule, or provide additional necessary information to the contractor as required under the contract provisions.

NOTE *It is important to ensure that there is no reasonably necessary information outstanding, general or specific. Watch the contractor's programme and progress for indicated dates and signs.*

NOTE *Deal with claims as empowered under the terms of the contract.*

SEE ALSO
K/SM5

Variations should be pre-priced if possible, otherwise the likely full implications should be estimated and agreed before action is taken.

It may be that negotiation is the best way forward, but do not exceed your authority. Do not be overawed by the volume of documents sometimes presented by claims consultants – quantity does not equate with the validity of a case.

Beware of claims regarding matters not dealt with under the express terms of the contract because the architect has no power to settle these; they must be dealt with between the parties.

NOTE *Issue instructions with respect to provisional sums and appointment of specialist subcontractors, etc.*

SEE ALSO
K/SM4

If possible, nominated or named subcontractors should be appointed at the commencement of the contract, always strictly in accordance with stipulated procedures. Note the subcontract dates for compatibility with the main contractor's programme.

K

ACTION **K274**	Issue certificates as empowered and required in accordance with the contract procedures. Request vouchers from the contractor as empowered under the contract.	SEE ALSO **K/SM6**
NOTE	*Be punctilious about valuations and certificates for payment. Notify the QS in writing of any work not properly carried out, so that such work is not included in any valuation. Alert the client to any rights to make a deduction from the amount certified, and the procedures involved.*	

NOTE	*Review the Health and Safety File information at regular intervals.*	

NOTE	*Maintain 'as built' records or drawings, as required under the contract provisions, and pass relevant information to the planning supervisor for possible incorporation in the Health and Safety File.*	SEE ALSO **K/SM4**

NOTE	*Check that the clerk of works and consultants maintain adequate records and pass relevant information to the planning supervisor for possible incorporation in the Health and Safety File.*	SEE ALSO **K/SM4**

ACTION **K275**	Obtain the contractor's forecast date for practical completion and advise the client of the procedures.	SEE ALSO **K/SM7**

ACTION **K276**	Remind the client of their responsibility for the building in terms of insurance, security and maintenance in good time.

ACTION **K277**	Initiate pre-completion checks on the works with the clerk of works and make records of outstanding items.
NOTE	*Any lists are for the benefit of the design team and the client, and not normally for issue to the contractor. Under JCT traditional forms, quality control on site, snagging, etc. is entirely the responsibility of the contractor.*

ACTION **K278**	When completion is near, make sure that the contractor is fully aware that commissioning must be completed and operating manuals available before the building is handed over.

ACTION **K279**	Identify responsibility for commissioning, testing and witnessing of engineering services and that it is carried out according to the provisions of the contract.

ACTION K280	Check that information relating to the Health and Safety File, maintenance manuals and operating instructions is complete and ready for handing over to the CDMC.
ACTION K281	Make sure that operating manuals have been properly checked and are ready by the time of handover.
ACTION K282	Cooperate with the CDMC, who will want to make sure that the Health and Safety File has been compiled and is ready at the time of handover.
ACTION K283	Issue the certificate of practical completion in accordance with the provisions of the contract.
NOTE	*Certify practical completion only when, in your opinion, this state has been attained. Be very wary of pressure from the contractor or client to certify practical completion early – the consequences can be serious for all concerned.*
ACTION K284	Hold a formal handover meeting, if terms of appointment or contract require it.

K290   Cost planning

ACTION K291	Liaise with the QS to monitor costs arising from architect's instructions, and for forecasting monthly reports.
ACTION K292	Provide the client with estimates of costs arising from architect's instructions, including variations.
ACTION K293	Notify the QS of any work against which monies must be withheld or where 'an appropriate deduction' is to be made from the contract sum.
ACTION K294	Liaise generally with the QS over remeasurement, valuations and the issue of monetary certificates, and applications for direct loss and/or expense.

ACTION **K295**	Deal with applications for reimbursement of direct loss and/or expense fairly and promptly.

ACTION **K296**	Report to the client on cost matters at agreed intervals.

K300   General Procedures

ACTION **K301**	Regularly check progress against the timetable for services.

ACTION **K302**	Continue resource control procedures for job (usually monthly): • Check expenditure against the office job cost allocation for Stage K. • Monitor fee income against projected fee income.

ACTION **K303** NOTE	Report regularly to the client on fees and expenses incurred, and submit accounts at agreed intervals (usually monthly). *Check that the client settles all accounts promptly.*

ACTION **K304**	Maintain accounts procedures for invoicing the contractor for copies of additional drawings and documents.

ACTION **K305**	Set up procedures to issue certificates and fee accounts regularly.

K400   Stage Outputs

Tangible results/material produced before the conclusion of Stage K might include the following:

- information (drawn and written), decisions and instructions (obligatory or discretionary), as necessary for the contractor to perform their obligations under the contract, issued during the progress of the works

- valuations (on minor works) and certificates (monetary and otherwise), issued in accordance with the contract, during the progress of the works

- records of all correspondence, instructions and certificates, and 'state of the art' documents, whether from manufacturers or other sources, which should be retained in case there are later disputes

- 'as built' drawings, manuals or other maintenance information required under the contract

- Health and Safety File information, as required under the CDM Regulations

- programmes for maintenance, if required

K

Supplementary Material

K/SM1: Keeping the client informed

The client will expect to be kept informed about the progress of work and given a regular report on the financial situation. Any material changes in design or construction will need prior approval.

How this is best handled will depend on the size of the job, the client's own organisation and the stipulated procedures for the project team. A few clients might prefer to leave matters almost entirely in the hands of the architect but the majority will expect formal reports at regular intervals. Some clients will expect to be directly represented at site progress meetings. Matters to be kept in mind include the following:

Time

The client will need to be kept informed about programme and progress. This information will be available through minutes of site progress meetings (issued by the architect), copies of correspondence relating to notices of delay, and the award of any extensions of time. It is particularly important that the client is kept informed about any anticipated change to the completion date or the construction cost, as this will have managerial and financial implications for the client.

Quality

The client will need to be kept informed about any problems concerning materials and workmanship where it becomes necessary to issue architect's instructions. The client should also be advised in good time about such matters as regular maintenance and the need to appoint or instruct staff about installation requirements, control and maintenance of systems. It might also be necessary for the client to take out maintenance contracts for certain installations.

Cost

The client should receive detailed statements of expenditure at regular intervals, with an appraisal of the current position and a forecast of total costs. The client must agree any extra expenditure in advance, whether this is for unavoidable adjustments in design or modifications requested by the client or an adjustment because of provisional sums expenditure. Where possible, it is good policy to have variations costed before the instruction is implemented. Cost reports will normally be prepared by the QS, but where no QS has been appointed (e.g. on minor works) these might have to be prepared by the architect.

For a typical financial report to client, see Fig. K1.

K/SM2: Site meetings

The usual procedure is for the architect to arrange and chair site progress meetings, and for the contractor to arrange and chair production meetings. In addition, the architect will call and chair special meetings including additional consultant team meetings for as long as the project requires this. There are also site inspections by the architect, which may or may not be formal and which may take place the same day as the site progress meeting.

As a general rule meetings should only be called for a clear purpose and should only involve those persons necessary for the successful conduct of the business. All meetings should be properly convened with a precise agenda issued in advance and be chaired in a firm and fair manner. All decisions should be clearly minuted.

Architect's/contract administrator's site progress meetings

These are essentially policy meetings and should take place at regular intervals (e.g. the first Tuesday in the month). It is sometimes helpful if they are immediately preceded by site visits but the two should be kept distinct as they serve entirely different purposes. The main business of the meetings will be to receive reports and to agree action necessary as a result. They are not the place to answer routine queries or provide general information. All the people who attend these meetings should have the authority to act.

A standard agenda of items should be maintained, and it is useful to include an 'Action' column. Minutes are normally issued by the architect/contract administrator – although this is sometimes done by the contractor, the architect/contract administrator should be alert to the fact that instructions contained in minutes prepared by the contractor or other person may not carry the same legal effect. Minutes should be issued soon after the meeting to all those named on the agreed distribution list. It is sensible to require that any dissent from the minutes is made in writing within seven days of issue.

For a specimen agenda, see Fig. K2.

Meetings for special purposes

Even with meetings called ad hoc for some special purpose there should be an agenda and a formal minute of decisions taken. Meetings might be needed for various reasons, for example with representatives of adjoining owners, or statutory bodies. It might also be necessary to convene further consultant team meetings during work on site and as long as they are needed a consistent agenda and format should be maintained. Such business should not be merged with the architect's/contract administrator's site progress meetings.

K

Contractor's production meetings

These are technical meetings with the subcontractors and are arranged by the contractor to take place before the architect/contract administrator progress meetings. The architect/contract administrator may be asked to attend; if so, they should make a note of any decisions and act appropriately. The contractor should prepare and distribute the minutes.

K/SM3: Site inspections

These are visits by the architect (as designer) to observe and comment on the contractor's site supervision and examples of work at intervals appropriate to the stage of construction. This is periodic inspection, which should be carried out to the extent determined by the nature of the work, and as agreed with the client in the appointing document. However, it should be noted that there is an obligation (reinforced by case law) for construction professionals to make visits to the site as necessary for the inspection of the works. Although the number of visits can be specified in the architect's agreement, this relates only to fees and if more visits are necessary they may be chargeable extras. If more frequent visits or constant inspection are required, then the client should be recommended to appoint a clerk of works or other resident site inspector. It should not be termed or thought of as 'supervision', because this suggests the authority to issue instructions to operatives, which clearly an architect does not possess.

Site visits should be spot checks made without prior warning but should have a specific purpose and as such require preparation beforehand. This might mean devising a plan after studying the most recent reports and minutes of meetings. The architect will then visit the site with the purpose of observing particular parts or items and of checking that specified tests are being carried out and verified. Checks of a general nature might include:

- whether quality complies generally with the provisions of the contract
- whether progress accords with the contractor's master programme
- whether essential parts of the design have been/are being carried out in accordance with the contract provisions

Such visits should be carried out carefully, and comments systematically noted. Where certificates refer to work, etc. 'properly executed', it is helpful to have a record of notes made at the time of a visit. Queries are often raised during site visits, and it may be prudent to reserve answers until returning to the office. Any decisions made or information given while on site should be confirmed in writing as soon as possible.

Reports of site visits should be prepared to a consistent format as soon after the visit as possible. Record photographs (dated), notes and sketches should be attached and carefully filed. These should be retained strictly for in-house use.

Fig. K3 is a specimen site visit report form.

K

K/SM4: Issuing instructions

Under most building contracts the only person authorised to issue instructions to the contractor will be the contract administrator. It is sensible to establish at the start of the job what constitutes an 'architect's instruction', and it is suggested that only written instructions issued on a standard form should be regarded as valid. The giving of oral instructions, using contractors' site instruction books, or taking the minutes of site meetings as instructions should all be avoided.

The particular form of contract used will state what powers are given to the contract administrator with regard to instructions, and only empowered instructions will bind the contractor. When issuing an instruction it is advisable to check the following:

- that it is empowered under the contract, and the relevant clause number can be cited
- that the identifying details are entered on the form (e.g. name of project, contractor, date of instruction, serial number, etc.)
- that the instructions are precisely worded and their meaning unambiguous
- that the instruction is signed by the authorised person

A file copy will be retained, and it is also good practice to keep a record of AIs issued for the project. See Fig. K4 for specimen form.

K/SM5: Dealing with claims

Although the word is frequently used, 'claim' is something of a misnomer as far as contract administration is concerned. The architect has the authority to act where the contract conditions expressly provide for entitlement in certain events, particularly concerning extensions of time and reimbursement of loss and expense.

Claims not expressly within the contract provisions or where, for various reasons, a contractor has elected not to follow the procedures or is unable to conform to the express terms, would be 'ex-contractual' claims to be pursued in arbitration or litigation.

Extensions of time

Most construction contracts include a mechanism for dealing in a convenient way with events which might affect progress, which are beyond the control of the contractor, and which were not foreseeable at the time of tender. For this to be operable there must be a clearly stated date for possession or commencement, and a date for completion. There is usually an extension of time provision and a separate provision for dealing with additional costs which might arise.

Extensions of time provisions benefit the contractor in that it is relieved of paying liquidated damages for failure to complete because of stated reasons. The express terms are also very much in the client's interests by keeping alive the right to liquidated damages even though the contract period is extended because of the client's intervention. It is, of course, essential that such intervention is included as an event covered in the contract conditions, and that the architect operates the extensions of time provisions strictly in accordance with the contract requirements.

When dealing with extensions of time, remember the following:

- Respond to each and every proper notice of delay from the contractor – at least this is evidence that the claim has been considered.
- When awarding extensions of time, do so only for the causes specified in the contract. State the causes but do not apportion. Keep full records in case the award is contested.
- Comply strictly with the procedural rules. For example, if the contract requires it, notify every nominated subcontractor of a decision.
- Observe the timescale if one is stated in the contract. If none is stated, act within a reasonable time.
- Form an opinion which is fair and reasonable in the light of the information available at the time.

K

Loss and/or expense applications

Monetary claims arising in the context of building contracts are usually made as a result of loss due to regular progress being affected or because of additional costs due to a prolongation of the time on site. The wording in the contract usually identifies events or matters which are recognised as causes. There may be procedures to be followed which exist for the convenience of both parties. It is only these types of claims which the architect administering the contract has the authority to settle.

For an application to be valid:

- the loss and/or expense must be a direct actual loss
- the works (or a part) must be materially affected
- interference or disturbance to regular planned progress must have occurred
- reimbursement must not be possible under any other contractual provision

The architect has a duty to decide whether the claim is valid and, if information supplied is not adequate, additional reasonably necessary information must be requested.

Ascertainment of the amount claimed can rest with the architect but normally the contract allows specifically for this function to be referred to the cost consultant.

When dealing with applications for reimbursement, remember the following:

- The object of these provisions is to put the contractor back into the position it would have been in but for the disruption. It is not an opportunity to profit.
- The contractor must make written application at the proper time.
- The architect must form an opinion about whether direct loss and/or expense has been incurred or is likely to be incurred, and that regular progress has been materially affected.
- The burden of proof rests with the contractor. If the notice is not sufficient, more information must be requested.
- Ascertainment is a matter of certainty and not approximation. Particularisation of claims, i.e. 'actual' figures relating to specific items, should be expected.

The importance of keeping good records cannot be emphasised enough.

It is recommended that a record should be kept of site delays observed or noted from reports; defective work observed which might relate to subsequent applications when instructions are issued; a schedule of 'claims' submitted by the contractor which need to be noted and acted upon. For specimen record forms, see Figs. K5, K6, and K7.

K/SM6: Issuing certificates

Contracts generally provide for the issue of certificates by the contract administrator. The issue will normally be an obligation, always subject to certain conditions being satisfied. A certificate is simply a statement of fact and although a letter might constitute a certificate, it is advisable to establish at the beginning of the job that valid certificates will be those issued on a standard form. Refer to the RIBA Contract Administration Forms Project Packs for guidance on use of the forms. Under the JCT Standard building contract SBC05 the following certificates are used:

Interim certificate

This is for payment to the contractor of an instalment of the contract sum. It might be on a monthly valuation (although the architect when certifying must use skill and care, and not blindly follow the cost consultant's valuation), on a stage or milestone basis as agreed by the parties and in accordance with the contract conditions.

Statement of Retention

These should be attached to the interim certificate and show the gross valuation of work done, identification of amounts subject to full retention, half retention and nil retention and the calculation of amounts of retention, which should be transferred to the interim certificate.

Sectional Completion Certificate

These are for use where the contract provides for the work to be carried out in phases.

Statement of Partial Possession by the employer

Where the contract makes provision for this, the employer may take possession of a part or parts of the works ahead of practical completion of the whole of the works. It requires agreement of the contractor which cannot be unreasonably withheld.

Notification of Revision to Completion Date

For use where an extension of time has been given, work has been omitted or in the final review following practical completion.

K

Non-Completion Certificate

A factual statement, upon which much may depend e.g. the deduction of liquidated damages by the employer, or the right to deduct damages by a main contractor against a nominated subcontractor, etc.

Practical completion certificate

A statement which expresses that the works have reached practical completion. The contractor is relieved from various obligations henceforth.

K/SM7: Preparing for handover

Although not usually referred to in building contracts, the process of completion and handing over the building should nevertheless be subject to careful planning and procedures. These should comprise:

- final commissioning, testing and witnessing of services installations
- pre-completion checks by the contract administrator
- preparation for the formal handing over
- issue of the practical completion certificate
- the formal handover meeting

Normally the contract administrator can expect to be advised by the contractor when the works are approaching practical completion. Sometimes this indication is premature. Sometimes the client will pressure the contract administrator to certify prematurely. The contract administrator should act strictly in accordance with the conditions of the contract. The parties are free to agree an expedient arrangement outside the contract terms if they so wish.

Final commissioning, testing and witnessing of services installation

Commissioning is the process whereby static completion of an installation is brought to the state of full working order for proving. Testing is a matter of checking a commissioned installation and evaluating its performance measured against specified requirements. Commissioning and testing are operations which, on a sophisticated project, might need to be carried out by specialists, will need to be effectively managed, and should be subject to a commissioning specification and system for commissioning. They might also need to be phased, and although the installations will need to be commissioned before handover, some adjustment and testing might not be possible until after installations have been in use for a certain period.

Almost every project includes a services installation, and proper thought is needed at the outset concerning design, installation, inspection and arrangements for commissioning and testing. Many larger client bodies expect particular codes to be observed and stated procedures to be followed. The Chartered Institution of Building Services Engineers publishes a series of Commissioning Codes which clearly itemise the checks necessary for various installations. The Building Services Research and Information Association publishes a guide to operating and maintenance manuals for building services installations. Reference to appropriate documents such as these will normally be made when specifying methods of commissioning.

K

Tender documents should clearly state the level of commissioning and testing which will be required, both before handover and additionally, perhaps, with a defects liability period of appropriate duration. Thought should also be given to the need for incorporating special conditions of contract because most standard forms do not make specific reference to such matters.

Where services installations are of a complex nature, it is likely that consultants and specialist firms will be involved, and expert commissioning engineers might need to be brought in. Nevertheless, the main contractor still has the responsibility for overall programming, and for ensuring that the works are finished by the contract completion date. This will usually necessitate commissioning, testing, and the preparation of operating or maintenance manuals before handover. Sometimes difficulties arise where these latter operations are not allocated sufficient time, or where the costs entailed have not been fully covered in the contract sum.

A common difficulty is the precise definition of responsibilities. Architects will obviously have a responsibility to see that requirements are properly included for and stated at the outset.

Manufacturers will also have a responsibility, particularly where use of particular components is specified. Inspection of services installations as work proceeds may be largely in the hands of consultants and subcontractors, although the main contractor will ultimately remain responsible for all matters of workmanship and materials. While architects will have a duty to see that appropriate arrangements are made for commissioning and testing, responsibility for carrying out such operations should clearly lie with others.

The following checklist can be used:

Pre-completion checks:

- Warn the contractor to make sure that the building is ready for inspection well before the date of practical completion.
- Instruct the clerk of works to maintain systematic preliminary inspections and to keep the architect informed of progress and any difficulties likely to arise as well as defects discovered.
- Check progress of building control and any other statutory approvals.
- Consolidate a schedule of outstanding items from:

  - the architect's progress meeting minutes
  - the consultants' reports
  - the clerk of works' reports
  - the architect's instructions
  - site visit notes

> NOTE
>
> *These lists are for communication between the consultants and for the architect's own records. They should not be issued to the contractor as quality control is the contractor's responsibility and the architect should not be drawn into taking on this role. If necessary, inform the contractor that the works are not complete according to the contract, and indicate general areas of concern. Remind the contractor to complete record drawings, etc. according to the agreed programme.*

Inspection and commissioning:

- In collaboration with consultants, advise the contractor and all subcontractors to coordinate a programme of checks.
- Instruct the clerk of works accordingly and ensure they check that defective work has been replaced and report any delays anticipated, where relevant asking the client's staff to attend inspections and checks.
- Ask the consultants to make detailed inspections and to report back.
- Check that the associated contractors' works are completed.
- Remind subcontractors to complete record drawings, etc. and to prepare maintenance instructions as agreed.
- Make formal arrangements with the client for handover inspections.
- Approve Document L compliance check.
- Confirm cleaning and maintenance measures under CDM regulations.

Preparation for the formal handover

Before the meeting:

- Remind the client of the reasonable standards which are appropriate to the class of work specified. It is the architect's/contract administrator's responsibility to certify.
- Inform the client's representative of the basis of the contract (if they have not been personally involved from the start).
- Write to the contractor and all those who are to attend the meeting to let them know the time, date and venue.

Inspecting the buildings and site:

- Hold meeting(s) for inspection and handover.
- Check that the following are ready to hand over as required:

  - building owner's operating manual
  - keys
  - 'as built' drawings
  - details of maintenance arrangements
  - Health and Safety File

K

- Outline the client's and contractor's responsibilities during the defects liability period.
- Outline arrangements for dealing with any future defects.
- Agree any additional works required by the client.

Additional works (if necessary):

- Liaise with the cost consultant and contractor to negotiate the basis for pricing.
- Prepare drawings and instructions and obtain the client's approval of these and the related costs.
- Instruct the contractor to proceed (by means of an extension of the contract, or a separate agreed instruction).
- Check that these are covered by the construction phase Health and Safety Plan.

Issue of the practical completion certificate

The practical completion certificate triggers a sequence of events, namely:

- The contractor's liability for damage to the completed works is ended.
- The contractor's liability for any further liquidated damages is ended.
- The contractor's liability for insurance of the works is ended.
- The contractor's liability for damage to the works as a result of frost is ended.
- Half the retention money is usually released to the contractor.

A practical completion certificate is issued only when in the opinion of the contract administrator (or other person referred to expressly in the contract) the works have reached a state of practical completion.

The formal handover meeting

The arrangements listed will be relevant in nearly all cases, including where there is sectional completion or partial possession.

Record attendance, date, etc.

Define purpose of meeting:

- Explain that inspections of building and site are to establish agreement that work is ready to hand over to the client for occupation.
- Note defects due to faulty workmanship or materials and issue instructions to the contractor to rectify them, immediately if appropriate.
- Ensure that all the contractor's plant and property have been removed from site.

Tour of inspection:

- Inspect building(s) and site.

Handover of building:

The client accepts the building and site from the contractor, and the contractor hands over the keys.

- Ensure that meters have been read and fuel stocks noted.

Maintenance manuals, servicing contracts, etc.:

- Confirm with the planning supervisor the contents of the Health and Safety File, and arrangements for delivering it to the client.
- Hand over any further building maintenance information as relevant, including:

  - directory
  - servicing contracts
  - maintenance of plant
  - maintenance of building
  - attention to landscape and planting
  - routine replacement schedules
  - record or 'as built' drawings as applicable

K

Figures

Figure K1: Specimen financial report to client

Job no: Job title:

Financial report to client

To end of (month)	(year)	Savings £	Extra £	£
Financial approvals	Contract sum as adjusted			
	Additional approvals to date of last report			
	Total approvals to date of last report			
Adjustments	Contract sum as adjusted including contingencies			
	Cost adjustment on PC sums ordered			
	Cost adjustment on provisional sums			
	Value of AIs issued to date			
	Changes of work anticipated			
Contingencies	Original contingencies sum			
	Estimated proportion absorbed to date			
	Estimated remainder			
Cost of works	Estimated cost of works including contingencies sum			
Reconcilliation	Variations instructed by the employer since last report			
	(a) [addition] estimated cost			
	(b) [omission] estimated saving			
	Additional approvals to last report			
Final estimate	Estimated final expenditure on present information			

Not included in assessments:
VAT, fees, other works (eg piling, landscape, advance orders)

Figure K2: Specimen agenda for architect's site progress meeting

Job no: Job title:

Agenda for site progress meeting

1   Minutes of last meeting

2   Contractor's report

- General report
- Sub-contractor's meeting report
- Progress and programme
- Causes of delay
- Health and Safety matters
- Information received since last meeting
- Information and drawings required
- Architect's instructions required

3   Clerk of works' report

- Site matters
- Quality control monitoring
- Lost time
- Tests observed and verified

4   Consultants' reports

- Structural works
- Mechanical works
- Electrical works

5   Quantity surveyor's report

6   Communications and procedures

7   Contract completion date

- Likely delays and their effect
- Review of factors from previous meeting
- Factors for review at next meeting
- Revision to completion date
- Revisions required to programme

8   Any other business

9   Date of next meeting

K

Figure K3: Specimen report form for predictive site visits

Job no: _____   Job title: _____

Site visit report

Date: _____   No. of visits scheduled: _____

Visit by: _____   Visit no.: _____

Purpose

_____
_____
_____
_____
_____
_____
_____
_____
_____
_____

Observed

_____
_____
_____
_____
_____
_____
_____
_____
_____
_____
_____
_____
_____
_____
_____
_____
_____
_____

Checked	**Recorded**
Samples	Photos
Verification of tests	
Vouchers	Video
Records	Other

Summary   Work properly executed ☐   Proceeding in workmanlike manner ☐

Materials properly stored and protected ☐   Progress to programme ☐

Figure K4: Specimen record form of architect's instructions issued

Job no:　　　　　　　Job title:

Architect's Instructions issued

Date	AI no.		Item	Subject	Estimated +/- cost (£)
	1		Gas main	Quotation ref 8438/63	+ 150
	2		Cills	Revised detail drawg. L.51/03	– 75
	3		Opening	First floor revised drawg. L51/12	+ 100
	4	(1)	Hip tiles	Omit farsand/ add Red Bank	+142
		(2)	Hip irons	Omit / add finials	

1. Use an AI for all instructions and notifications to the contractor.

2. List all individual items in any AI.

3. Make sure all instructions are clearly worded and unambiguous.

4. Do not reserve numbers for future issues; do not miss out any numbers. If any error in numbering is found, immediately notify everyone on the distribution list.

K

Figure K5: Specimen record form of site delays observed

Job no: Job title:

Record of site delays observed

Date	Delay	Item	Reason	Observed by
6.1.95	1 week	Site clearance	Plant hire equipment late	C of W
17.1.95	1 week	Weather	Heavy snow	C of W
23.2.95	3 days	Foundations	Excavations waterlogged	C of W
10.4.95	2 days	Steelworks	Erectors arrived	H R J
			Problem with crane jib	
			Left site	

1. Record observations in sequence of work element/location, conditions or situation and note the source of information where relevant.

2. Liaise closely with clerk of works and consultants.

3. Check against and coordinate with your site inspection reports.

Figure K6: Specimen record form of defective work

Job no: Job title:

Record of defective work

Date	Item	Contractor notified (date)	Value if deducted (£)	Cleared (date)
1.8.95	Priming to some steelwork unsatisfactory	2.8.95		2.9.95
16.9.95	Nosing to boiler house steps not satisfactory, shuttering poor	16.9.95		12.10.95

1. Describe the work in sequence of work element/location; condition as rejected; rectification required.

2. Check and update this record regularly with clerk of works and consultants.

3. Notify QS of any values deducted against valuations made and when items are cleared.

4. Check against and coordinate with your site inspection reports.

K

Figure K7: Specimen schedule of claims by contractor

Job no: Job title:

Schedule of claims by contractor

| Date | Clause no. | Item | Time/amount: | | Date for decision | Date awarded |
			Req'std	Allowed		
25.2.95	25	Weather — notice of delay				
		inadequate — more detailed				
		information requested				
		AI No. 1				
	25	Gas main	4 days	2 days		
	26	Consequential loss/expense				

1. Check that contractor uses procedures laid down in the contract.

2. Inform QS, consultants, clerk of works immediately any claim is notified.

3. List adequate description and if neccessary open a sub-file to collate the correspondence etc about each claim.

4. Check that your action complies with the time limits stated in the contract.

Post Practical Completion

STAGE DESCRIPTION

As defined in *RIBA Outline Plan of Work 2007*:

L1 Administration of the building contract after practical completion and making final inspections

L2 Assisting building user during initial occupation period

L3 Post-occupation evaluation – review of project performance in use

CONTENTS

L

Stage Description

Stage L1 – After practical completion

At practical completion the client takes possession of the building, half of any retention money is released, and the contractor's liability for liquidated damages ends. There is generally a 12-month defects liability period (DLP) which commences at the date of practical completion and during which time the contractor must rectify any defects arising if instructed to do so. At the end of the DLP, the contractor must make good any remaining defects within a reasonable period of time. Upon completion of the making good of defects all retention money must be released and when all outstanding contractual issues have been resolved, the Final Certificate can be issued. This marks the conclusion of the contract.

Stage L2 – Initial occupation period

Stages L2 and L3 are additional services and, where they form part of the appointment, certain activities must be carried out from the outset of the project.

At Stage L2 the architect should make visits to site to make structured transfer of information to the users and the facilities management team, spot emerging issues and solve problems, and establish a method of providing ongoing assistance for the users.

The post-handover period is the most neglected stage of construction. Learning from how buildings perform in use – and fine-tuning them to perform better – remain central to the systematic improvement of the end product.

Continuous commissioning, as suggested in BRE Digest 474, to fine-tune the building and rectify any faults will help provide the building occupier with peace of mind and increase customer satisfaction. If teething troubles are ironed out through fine-tuning, the building will run more efficiently and save the building user time and money.

These processes are sometimes described as 'sea trials' or 'soft landing'. A useful reference is www.usablebuildings.co.uk.

Stage L3 – Post-occupation evaluation

On completion of a project there will always be the need to assemble documents for retention, and to compile records. This is an activity appropriate to nearly all projects. A study of such material could lead to an updating of the office systems to take account of lessons learned. There are then three levels at which further post-completion studies may be carried out.

First, there could be an investigation or appraisal restricted to an in-house operation. Second, there could be a debriefing exercise which could involve other people concerned with the project, and this could commence shortly after completion. Third, there could be a full post-occupancy evaluation which would normally occour at least one or two years after Practical Completion in order to obtain reliable data.

Both in-house appraisals and debriefing are exercises not normally listed in the services provided by the architect and are unlikely to be funded by the client. However, they can provide useful lessons for the members of both the design team and the construction team.

A full feedback study can be costly and if the client wishes this to be undertaken, it will probably have to be the subject of a separate commission. With partnering arrangements it is likely to be an essential part of assessing whatever targets have been set. Full post-occupancy evaluations can be particularly useful to clients who construct more than once, in order to improve the briefing they provide for future projects. However, it is a sensitive area and confrontation should be avoided at all costs. The architect's professional indemnity insurers should be informed before a full feedback study is undertaken for the client.

Key Obligations

(from RIBA Agreements 2007: Standard Agreements (S-Con-07): Schedule of Design Services (SS-DS-07))

L1

Advise on resolution of defects.

Provide information for agreeing final account.

L2

Assist building user during initial occupation period, if applicable.

L3

Carry out post-occupation evaluation, if applicable.

L

L100	Preliminary Issues

L(1)110	Information required (L1)

Check that all information necessary during Stage L1 is available, which might include the following:

- copies of the Health and Safety Plan developed by the CDMC
- sets of administration forms appropriate for the form of contract being used
- Energy Performance Certificate

L(2)110	Information required (L2)

As-installed information for services, construction detailing, etc, (if have responsibility for producing the Energy Performance Certificate).

Brief from the occupier on their operational requirements.

Building log book.

L(3)110	Information required (L3)

Energy use data, e.g. utilities bills.

L(1)120	**Appointment (L1)**

ACTION **L(1)121**	Establish scope, content and context for Stage L activities.
NOTE	*Put it into context, particularly if previous stages were undertaken by others. If possible establish whether material produced now is likely to be acted upon by others taking over subsequent stages.*

ACTION **L(1)122**	If coming new to the project at this stage in the Plan of Work:
	• Ascertain that the relevant Pre-Agreement and earlier stage checks have been carried out.
NOTE	*Allow for familiarisation and reviewing of all usable material when agreeing fees and timetable with the client.*
	• *Confirm the role of the architect in relation to the rest of the consultant team.*
	• *Ensure that you have adequate professional indemnity insurance cover.*

ACTION **L(1)123**	Check the client's written instruction to proceed.

ACTION **L(1)124**	Check that the client has settled all accounts submitted to date.

ACTION **L(1)125**	Check appointing documents with respect to services and fees.
	• If the services, cost or time targets are different from the agreement with the client, agree a formal variation by letter or deed, as appropriate.
	• If the extent of professional services for Stage L1 is not yet settled, agree with the client and confirm in writing.
NOTE	*Remember that the agreed services must reflect the role of the architect under the form of building contract selected. Inform the client in advance if more frequent visits are required than those allowed for in the agreement and which would incur additional expenditure.*

L

ACTION **L(1)126**	Assess office resources needed for Stage L1 and ensure that they are available and adequate.

ACTION **L(1)127**	If accredited for EPC administration, check if the client wants to instruct this and if so agree fees.

For information of EPCs refer to the government website www.communities.gov.uk/planningandbuilding/theenvironment/energyperformancecertificates.

Energy Performance Certificates are required for all buildings when they are constructed, leased or sold. In newly constructed or refurbished buildings it will normally be provided by the main contractor. For clarification on exceptions for providing EPCs and what they should cover, refer to the relevant guide in www.communities.gov.uk.

L(2)120   Appointment (L2)

ACTION **L(2)121**	Check if the client wants to instruct the design team to undertake continuous commissioning, 'sea trials' and 'soft landings', etc. and if so agree a scope of service for the additional service and fee. Agreement for this service should be confirmed prior to going to tender.

A soft landings team (designer and builder) is resident on site during the move-in period to deal with emerging issues more effectively. It can then monitor building use and energy performance for the first two to three years of occupation, identifying opportunities both for fine-tuning the building and for improvements in future developments. The process also creates a coordinated route to post-occupancy evaluation (POE).

NOTE	*Sea trials are where the design team are involved in running the building for the first two years.*

ACTION **L(2)122**	If a BREEAM 2008 Assessment has been commissioned you may need to provide information to the BREEAM assessor in order to allow him to complete the post-occupancy stage of the assessment.
NOTE	*A BREEAM 2008 Certificate will not be issued until after the post completion stage of the assessment has been completed. For further guidance refer to www.breeam.org.*

L(3)120   Appointment (L3)

ACTION **L(3)121**	Check to see if the client wishes to undertake a BREEAM In Use: 2008 assessment of the building in operation, for the building type, and agree scope of the service and fee.
ACTION **L(3)122**	Check if the client wants to instruct a post-occupancy evaluation exercise and if so agree the scope of service and the fee with the client.
ACTION **L(3)123**	Advise the client of the need to employ other consultants and the contractor.

L(1)130   Client (L1)

ACTION **L(1)131**	Remind the client that responsibility for insurance reverts to them.

L

L(2)130	**Client (L2)**
ACTION **L(2)131**	Check whether the client has issued an instruction for an Energy Performance Certificate prior to selling or leasing the building.

L(3)130	**Client (L3)**
ACTION **L(3)131**	If a full feedback study is planned, agree with the client what access will be available, what the timescale should be, and in what form the findings should be presented.
ACTION **L(3)132**	If the building is occupied by a public authority or an institution providing a public service to a large number of persons, with a total useful area greater than 1000m², check if the client has issued an instruction for a Display Energy Certificate.
ACTION **L(3)133**	Explain to the client the purpose of a debriefing exercise or POE and that their feedback might be a key part of this activity. Discuss to what extent key persons in the organisation could be expected to contribute opinions at a meeting chaired by the architect (see BRE Digest 478 for guidance).
ACTION **L(3)134**	Arrange a meeting with key personnel from the client organisation (the building users and maintenance staff). Ensure that you have considered your objectives and what information you want to get from this exercise and have a clear agenda for the meeting.
ACTION **L(3)135**	Discuss with the client to what extent the managers and users of the project could be expected to cooperate in completing a questionnaire.
ACTION **L(3)136**	Discuss with the client whether authorised photographers would be allowed access after final completion, for feedback purposes.

| ACTION L(3)137 | Discuss with the client whether it would be permissible for the architect to carry out a survey of the building in use some time after completion. | |
| ACTION L(3)138 | Check with your insurers that you have cover for feedback activities. | |

L200	**Stage Activities**

L(1)210	**(L1)**

ACTION L(1)211	Administer the terms of the building contract.	
ACTION L(1)212	Report to the client as appropriate.	
ACTION L(1)213	Collate all documents issued to the contractor, and store them.	SEE ALSO **L/SM1**
ACTION L(1)214	Collate 'state of the art' trade information, etc., and store it.	
NOTE	*Preparation of 'as built' drawings and maintenance manuals are included already under Stage K.*	
ACTION L(1)215	Conduct in-house appraisal of office performance on project.	SEE ALSO **L/SM2**
ACTION L(1)216	Consider holding a debriefing exercise with the client and other consultants.	SEE ALSO **L/SM3**

ACTION L(1)217	Check if the Building Log Book for the building operator – required by the Building Regulations – has been issued. The Building Log Book should be in accordance with the requirements of CIBSE TM31 (go to www.cibse.org).
ACTION L(1)218	Participate in the creation of Operating Manuals for the building. See BSRIA Technical Note TN15/95 for recommended contents of these manuals (go to www.bsria.co.uk).

L(2)210   (L2)

ACTION L(2)211	For residential schemes where the Code for Sustainable Homes is required, complete the post construction review of the CSH assessment so that 'final' code certification can be issued.
ACTION L(2)212	For non-domestic buildings undertake the post completion stage of the BREEAM assessment if required.
ACTION L(2)213	Provide a copy of a building user guide, if required, that contains the information that will be relevant to the non-technical building user to explain how the building systems operate to increase comfort levels etc. This might include an on-site presentation if required.
ACTION L(2)214	Seasonal commissioning to be undertaken so HVAC systems are commissioned for both summer and winter conditions, as agreed with client
ACTION L(2)215	Debriefing and feedback are management exercises. If it is agreed to extend the commission to include these, establish the scope and content of Stages L2 and L3.
NOTE	*Do not allow an exercise to be undertaken if it seems likely that it might result in recriminations – and even arbitration or litigation.* *Always inform your professional indemnity insurers before embarking on any feedback study.*

ACTION L(2)216	Check whether the design and production teams would cooperate in debriefing.

ACTION L(2)217	Check whether the client would cooperate in debriefing.
NOTE	*In-house appraisal is a healthy operation for nearly all projects, but participants must feel able to exchange views freely. Debriefing can become a sensitive matter and will only succeed with the full cooperation of all involved.*

ACTION L(2)218	Raise with all consultants the desirability of engaging in a systematic analysis of the management, construction and performance of the project.	SEE ALSO **L/SM4**

ACTION L(2)219	Arrange a series of debriefing meetings.

ACTION L(2)220	Convene debriefing meetings upon completion to evaluate technical matters, to involve all design team members, the main contractor and possibly the client.
NOTE	*At debriefing meetings, watch out for partisan or defensive attitudes.*
	Honest and objective discussion should not be allowed to degenerate into acrimony.

ACTION L(2)221	Record the discussions.

ACTION L(2)222	Formulate overall conclusions from the debriefing.

ACTION L(2)223	Make visits to the site to make a structured transfer of information to the users and the facilities management team.

ACTION L(2)224	Spot emerging issues and solve any problems arising.

ACTION L(2)225	Establish a method of providing ongoing assistance to the users.

L

L(3)210	(L3)
ACTION L(3)211	Consider the desirability of a full feedback study or a post-occupancy evaluation.
ACTION L(3)212	Year 1 Recalculate capital and revenue target costs at current rates. Identify the actual capital costs
ACTION L(3)213	Year 2 (and 3) Identify/provide data required for the review. Agree a programme of meetings. Identify the issues, establish causation and consider remedies. Contribute to the output reports and recommendations. If instructed, implement the recommendations.
ACTION L(3)214	Participate in the BREEAM In Use Assessment process if required.

NOTE *For further advice refer to www.usablebuildings.co.uk*

L400   Stage Outputs

Check that all the agreed outputs have been produced, which might include the following:

L(1)410   L1

- Certificate of Making Good of Defects

NOTE

This is issued when defects listed at the end of the defects liability period have been remedied.

- Final Certificate

NOTE

The issue of the final certificate brings the authority of the contract administrator, under the terms of the building contract, to a close. The contractor's liability continues, of course, until the end of the limitation period.

There might, in addition or alternatively, be contract provisions which refer to statements issued by the contract administrator or by the employer (e.g. in the case of design and build contracts). These should be regarded as requiring the same care and consideration as certificates before being issued. Case law has confirmed that there is no immunity from negligence in certifying.

L(2)410   L2

- EPCs

- Manual/building user guide, if part of scope

- Records of trials and their recommendations

L

L(3)410 | **L3**

- Record of conclusions reached at debriefing meetings, distributed to participants

- Results of full feedback study conducted with client or user client, or everyday users of the building, perhaps several years post-completion

NOTE

It is essential that the benefits and lessons learned from appraisals are passed to all members of staff. The office quality plan, manuals and procedures might need amendment or revision as a result.

Supplementary Material

L/SM1: Keeping office records

Once a job is complete, a decision has to be made about which drawings and documents should be kept. No office has the space to keep all project records indefinitely.

A set of project records, properly maintained and completed, should be a useful condensed history of the project – a point of reference for quick comparison of working methods, timescales and costs. Photographs of the work in progress and as completed, presentation drawings and models should also be kept available for prospective clients and for general publicity purposes. However, it is essential to keep proper records of the kind of information that will be required in the event of disputes, in particular:

- the client brief and related correspondence
- the contract documents
- architect's instructions
- minutes of project meetings
- certificates issued
- notes of inspections and surveys
- any crucial 'state of the art' information (manufacturers' key information, current BSs, Codes, etc.)
- progress charts, etc.
- selected working drawings

It is important to remember that the personnel involved with the project may not be available to give evidence if litigation occurs some years later.

L

L/SM2: In-house appraisal

Appraise the project under the headings given in the following checklist:

1. Office costs:

    - Relate office costs to reserve and profit targets.

2. Performance of design team, site inspectorate in terms of:

    - communications with client
    - communications between design team members
    - communications with CDM coordinator
    - communications with contractor
    - design team programming
    - quality of drawings, specifications
    - cost planning, final costs against budget
    - quality control
    - energy effectiveness
    - meeting completion date(s), etc.

3. Contractor's performance in terms of:

    - project management, quality of staff
    - site management, quality of staff
    - health and safety compliance
    - continuity of personnel
    - quality of work
    - effectiveness of programming
    - cooperation in settling claims
    - cooperation over material for Health and Safety File

4. Working arrangements between design team and contractor in terms of:

    - architect's progress meetings, actions on minutes
    - quality control
    - early identification of problems relating to progress, information and quality
    - potential disputes
    - financial arrangements, certificates, dayworks and measurement evaluation

5. Completed works in terms of:

    - resolution of the brief
    - relation to site and surroundings
    - quality of building, functional and abstract

- incorporation of M & E services into structure
- energy efficiency
- wear and tear, maintenance

6. Prepare reports:

- Include proposals for long-term reviews; distribute, file as appropriate.

7. Complete project records:

- Collect all relevant project records and information.
- Collate material and keep available for quick reference and comparison with that of other completed jobs.
- Arrange photographs for record and/or promotional purposes.

L

L/SM3: Debriefing

Obtaining valuable lessons with the benefit of hindsight is will not be an activity commissioned by every client, but it is a worthwhile exercise and, for a truly objective report, impartial 'auditors' could be engaged.

Debriefing after completion is something which should happen in all major projects to some extent. A series of meetings convened by the architect who acted as lead consultant could achieve this, as follows:

- meetings between the architect and CDMC to evaluate matters related to compliance with the CDM Regulations
- meetings between key design team members and the contractor to evaluate design and technical aspects of the project
- meetings between the architect and contractor to evaluate the management of the construction of the project.

A frank exchange of views might be expected at meetings, and the success of the operation will depend very much on the cooperation of all parties involved. Opinions on, for example, the overall timescale, the effectiveness of cost control, whether AIs including variations could have been avoided, whether drawings production and issue could have been improved, whether site reporting and quality control were effective, etc., might provide valuable lessons for future projects. Obviously the time spent on this kind of operation and the cost of meetings has to be weighed against the fact that the project is usually a 'once only' occurrence, and the particular team might never again be assembled. However, for 'repeat' clients and consultant teams, this exercise will be very useful in establishing working relations for future projects.

L/SM4: Post-occupancy evaluation

The more intensive investigations for feedback, which might not be practicable until one or two years after completion of the project, could include structured interviews with the client's staff or with users, access to the buildings, and access to information and records held by various team members.

Neither of these kinds of activities should be attempted if there is a risk of inviting acrimony and dispute, although there is significant potential value in terms of continued client relations, learning from feedback and aiding continuous improvement.

The purpose of a post-project evaluation is to analyse the management, construction and performance of a project. This could entail:

- an analysis of the project records
- an inspection of the fabric of the completed building
- studies of the building in use
- meetings and workshops with the client, consultants and users.

A post-project evaluation should cover:

- the purpose of the study
- the description of the need
- performance against cost, quality and timescale targets
- client satisfaction with the project and the facility
- user satisfaction with the facility
- performance and communications between project participants

  - project sponsor
  - client project manager
  - where relevant, client adviser
  - project team

- overview and recommendations

  - lessons learned
  - major points of action
  - costs

- technical appendices

  - user survey data
  - monitoring data
  - energy consumption, water use, etc.

L

Bibliography